BACK
TO THE
DAMN SOIL

BACK
TO THE
DAMN SOIL

MARY GUBSER
AND NICHOLAS J. GUBSER

PUBLISHED BY COUNCIL
OAK BOOKS, LTD. TULSA,
OKLAHOMA 1 9 8 6

COUNCIL OAK BOOKS, LTD.
1428 SOUTH ST. LOUIS
TULSA, OKLAHOMA 74120

PRINTED IN THE UNITED STATES OF AMERICA

LIBRARY OF CONGRESS CATALOG NUMBER 86-061319
ISBN 0-933031-06-8

DESIGNED BY CAROL HARALSON

FOR OUR FAMILY

ONE

DUST IN YOUR EYE, 1937

"Does this road go anywhere?" I asked.

"Of course," replied my husband. Gene had been unusually quiet as we turned off the main highway. Now he was carefully negotiating an unpaved, rough road full of rocks and holes. We were way out somewhere in the country far from the city. I wasn't exactly lost, but I needed reassurance. A few days ago we had celebrated my twenty-first birthday and three whole months of marriage. I took a quick glance at my husband. Never had I seen him with such a stern, set face. I was beginning to wonder what I was doing with this strange man out here in a primeval part of the world. I decided to venture another question.

"Where are we going?"

"You'll see."

I didn't have the nerve to say another word. After all, Gene was a dignified and mature man of twenty-four.

The dirt road suddenly came to an end. Looking out from the top of a little hill, I saw nothing except sun-bleached rocks. I couldn't believe roads came to an end — I thought they always circled back somewhere.

"It's windy," I said. "And dusty." I tied a scarf over my hair and got out of the car. My husband was looking out over this barren hill with a misty expression on his face.

Everywhere I looked were rocks. Then I saw a sign of life — two small weeds struggling against the wind. I looked up, over the horizon. This, I vaguely recognized, was what they called "bald prairie." Down the hill a little way I could see a suggestion of grass. It was thin and colorless. I'd seen golden ripe wheat rippling in the wind before, but this wasn't it. This was an empty expanse of weak, scraggly grass, parched to starvation.

"We're going to live here," announced my husband with quiet, unmovable determination.

My heart fell. "Here?" I squeaked, my wind-whipped eyes filling with tears. "In what? A tent? A dugout?"

"We'll build a house," he said. "This rock will make a solid foundation."

"Oh good," I said, dabbing at my dust-filled eyes. "Can we plant a few telephone poles . . . just to break up the view?"

My husband seemed oblivious to the horror that gripped me. I tried to calm myself. "The road out here will tear up our nice little car in another four or five trips," I said hopefully.

He turned to look at our car. It was a 1934 Willis coupé that he'd purchased for fifty dollars from an elderly uncle. It was black when he got it, two weeks before we were married. With his usual care and reasoning, he painted it a cream color — to match our Oklahoma dust, I guess. I was quite impressed that the paint job wasn't streaked through like a zebra. Most paint jobs in 1937 looked like "loving hands at home," with the brush marks plainly visible.

"Let me show you something," said my brand-new husband. He walked to the back of our Willis, opened the tiny trunk, and pointed to a small metal box.

"Fishing stuff?" I asked hesitantly.

"No," he laughed. "Tools. If the car breaks down, I can fix it."

I nodded, trying to show wifely appreciation for my husband's talents. "The problem," I said quietly, "is fixing this land."

That rocky hill was in Tulsa County just east of the city. That rutted dirt road we bumped over now has a name, Latimer Street. In

1937, there were only six or seven families within a square mile, eking out a Tobacco Road existence. From the top of our little hill on out east past the section line called Memorial Drive, there was a big, fat *nothing* — just Oklahoma as far as the dust would let you see. A few stunted willows outlined a tiny creek bed that twisted through the rocky terrain. All else was bald prairie. From the top of our hill, I would later learn, we could watch sandstorms blow in. It was a frightening experience to see the wind tear up dry earth, throw sand and dirt a mile into the sky, and obscure the sun until darkness closed in almost like the dusk of evening.

In our cream-colored Willis coupé, we headed back into the security of the city.

"It's our turn to go back to the soil," lectured my husband. "I'm a city boy, you're a city girl, but even so we can't deny the agrarian ideal that pushed this country from east to west."

I listened, as always. But passively, with skepticism. Yes, my husband had been born and had lived all his life in the same house in the city of Tulsa. His father had escaped from the soil in Missouri to become a lawyer in territorial Oklahoma, first county judge of Tulsa County, and eventually a distinguished lawyer and civic leader. I had always suspected that the Judge's early years on the land, shrouded in stories and myth, had a grip on my intense young husband. Now I no longer suspected — I knew.

Was I a city girl? That was a hard label for me to accept. I'm a PK — a Methodist preacher's kid. Growing up, I'd spent two to four years in nearly every town in Oklahoma — Heavener, Tulsa, Pauls Valley, McAlester, Duncan, Frederick — you name it. Really I was a small-town girl. My father enjoyed living in little towns where he could know everybody.

His formal education had screeched to a poverty-stricken halt in the fourth grade. He and his family were refugees from Georgia after the Civil War. They settled in east Texas, and at the age of ten my father signed on as a ranch hand to help support his family. He became an insatiable reader, left ranching as soon as he could, and was teaching country school at seventeen.

Several years later, he entered the ministry as a Methodist preacher — he loved the word *preacher*, for that's exactly what he felt he was called to be. He soon married one of his former students, who continued to call him "Mr. Douglass" long after the wedding.

My mother was a good cook with nothing in the pot. Occasionally when our larder was almost empty, we'd get a "pounding." What fun they were! A group from the church would gather for a surprise party, and each family would bring a pound of food. As everything was piled high on our dining room table, I would circle greedily, looking over the loot. I was a growing girl with a very healthy appetite. What a delight it was to see a pound each of sugar, bacon, canned peaches, occasionally fresh fruit, and always a pound of black-eyed peas and maybe a ham hock thrown in. A pounding brought friends together, and when things were really bad, we might have two or three parties a month. Everyone played games and had a hilarious time with no money spent. My father gloried in being the center of attention. He was a natural — part actor, part politician, and part teacher.

When someone generously put a bushel of green beans on our front porch during the spring and summer, my mother canned them in glass jars. She was always canning something and would tackle everything from okra to rabbits shot by my father. I dreaded canning days, for that meant I had to sit and string beans or peel tomatoes for hours on end. I would much rather sit on the back-porch steps and watch my father skin a squirrel or watch a tramp eat all our leftovers. Two or three tramps appeared every week at our back door, for those were the days before government welfare and the tramps all headed for the parsonage. My mother would heap a plate with hot food, pour a steaming cup of coffee, and take the meal out to the tramp on the back steps. No tramp was ever allowed inside the house, but my father would go out to join him on the steps, and I would follow, sitting close to my father to absorb the conversation. With good, hot food in his stomach, the tramp willingly revealed all his life and troubles. My father never attempted to convert him, but just listened to his story.

Growing up in a parsonage, I learned more than one trick for making do with limited funds. A girl I knew who wasn't allowed to wear lipstick dyed her lips with iodine. The stain didn't come off for two weeks. After that episode, my mother became much more

4

tolerant of my desire to imitate the habits of other maturing girls. But cosmetics were expensive. My sister helped me save pennies for three-cent stamps. Then I sent off for every free sample offered in newspapers and magazines. What fun it was to receive all those tiny boxes and jars and bottles! I had drawers filled with miniature containers of cleansing cream, powder, Mentholatum, lipsticks, vanishing cream, Cuticura ointment, rouge, and creams to bleach freckles (my sister thought buttermilk was the best solution).

My father wanted to expand my horizons beyond small-town life, so I was soon packed off to college. When I brought home news of my studies, my father startled me with his strong preference for Aeschylus over Sophocles and Euripides and with his great personal interest in Kant. Clearly my father had overcome the limitations of a fourth-grade education.

Both my parents wanted me to teach school before marrying, so I worked for five months as a substitute (the only job I could find) in a small town. I received the grand salary of fifty dollars a month. One month I got only forty-three of those precious dollars because I caught a nasty cold from one of my students. My illness required a substitute for the substitute, and I was docked seven dollars. A visit to the doctor cost me two dollars, so I only netted forty-one dollars that month. But I could keep all of it; there was no social security and no income tax for that amount. Twenty dollars paid my room and board each month. The rest I could fluff off as frivolously as I wished.

My one vice was an occasional cigarette. This I was allowed to have in the bathroom where I boarded. One evening three teachers invited me to their boardinghouse. Carefully the doors were closed. All four of us lighted up, puffed guiltily, then stubbed out the cigarettes in a special box with a tight lid. Our hostess brushed her teeth and gargled with mouthwash. I never knew what she did with the refuse in the box. For me, that strange evening put a complete damper on a life in the teaching profession.

The end of my glorious career as a teacher came as an immense relief. One semester in the Bible Belt was more than enough. All I had to show after those five strict months was two dollars. When I married Gene, my trousseau and dowry consisted of three mother-made dresses, one store-bought dress, my two dollars, and me.

In some ways, though, my new husband had a rougher time of it than I. He had entered the University of Chicago at sixteen on a scholarship, but his father's declining health and Depression-decimated family business forced him out of college after two years. This was a bitter blow. Then in 1936 the harshest blow came when his father died.

True, we were both urban people, and I felt I was almost sophisticated. I could not see any reason why *I* had to return to the damn soil. Still, I couldn't deny the grip that poor old piece of land had on my husband.

Our tiny first apartment in Tulsa had been a grim enough place when we moved in. The worst feature of all was a large painting entitled *The Lone Wolf* that loomed out at us from over the mantelpiece. This was a Depression portrait. A solitary, starving wolf huddled against a rock on a snowy hillside, its tail between its legs. A relentless wind beat without mercy at the craven animal. The wolf's eyes were almost human. They were filled with terror, epitomizing the worst of the Great Depression.

I wasn't ready for *The Lone Wolf.* Maybe we had our own rocky hillside to contend with, but we were hardly whipped curs. My first decorating achievement for our small home was to stick that picture into our one closet, wolf to the wall.

My second effort at redecorating was to arrange our first purchase, the *Encyclopedia Britannica,* across the mantel. The Harvard Classics, which were part of the bargain when we bought the encyclopedia, were piled on the floor. Thick law books adorned our dining table, for Gene was in his last year of law school, attending classes at night. With my three new cookbooks, we were settled. During the day my husband fought the battle of the Depression with plenty of company. Most everyone seemed to be having reversals, including us. But that never bothered me, for as a Methodist PK, I was used to being constantly in reverse — financially, that is.

Our household finances were such that we could just afford an occasional bottle of bootleg Scotch, but not a larger apartment. I never quite understood how Gene earned money. He seemed to bring in a few dollars here and there. All I knew was that we were making it, but only by a narrow margin.

I was about to learn how narrow. "We do have a problem out there," confessed my husband.

"Problem? Out where?" I asked.

"The land — our twenty-two acres."

"What is an acre, exactly?"

Gene exploded. All had been love and patience until now. I sat up at attention, ready for the next sermon — I mean lecture.

"An acre," he burst out, "is a parcel of land! A little over 40,000 square feet. There are 640 acres to a square mile!"

"Oh, then you have twenty-two of those," I said brightly, striving to maintain peace.

"Yes! Or maybe I have them. It's all a question of taxes."

I frowned. I sighed. I was ready to give up. As a preacher's daughter and girl-child of my generation, I was never meant to understand taxes.

"Taxes are fairly simple," my husband explained, trying to be conciliatory. "My father acquired those twenty-two acres a long time ago in settlement for a debt. After a few years, the property taxes started to be a burden. He decided to let the land go to the county, but I wanted to try raising chickens, so he deeded the property to me. My idea was to make enough money raising chickens to pay the taxes. But I got married instead."

"Good choice!" I said, laughing. But the early death of my father-in-law was still a dark cloud. Perhaps we should save the land for his sake. I decided to ponder this tough question on my own. The power of sentiment can be overwhelming — sometimes for good, sometimes not. I was troubled that the twenty-two acres were so worthless that my father-in-law had decided to abandon the property to the county. Didn't this mean that Gene's decision to keep the land might be a little off-base?

Late that night I said a little prayer. Being a PK can be hazardous to one's spiritual health. Long ago I had been turned off by the hypocritical politicking that raises its ugly head in some congregations. But I still trusted God. Now more than ever. If the taxes weren't paid, I prayed that the county officials would hold true to their duty and take those twenty-two acres.

Fortunately we were too busy to worry about moving out to that desolate hillside. My husband was thoroughly engrossed in finishing law school and keeping our household economy afloat. Of course, I became pregnant.

From today's viewpoint, that might seem like a tragic blow. How much worse could things get in an already desperate situation? But attitudes were different then. In the darkness that surrounded our lives, children and family and love provided the light. Sounds awfully sentimental, doesn't it? But I must confess, my opinion hasn't changed much.

Getting pregnant seemed a normal, logical occurrence to me, but not to my husband. He was ecstatic. After listening to his impassioned soliloquy of joy for over an hour, I was startled to hear him conclude, "And this child is all the more reason why we have to move out on the farm."

For a brief instant I had second thoughts about the wisdom of my pregnancy. But it was a little late to turn back now.

I had my own visions of what country life was all about. Uncle Alvah was the first real farmer I ever met. When I was seven years of age and he was sixty, Uncle Alvah decided to leave his farm in Arkansas for the first time and brave the outer world by making a train journey to visit his young half-brother, my father. He had made only one other big trip, when he left Georgia as a young boy in a covered wagon with his mother and two brothers. The mother remarried, moved to east Texas and raised a second family. The three brothers in turn moved to Arkansas, found the Ozark Mountains, and established farms near each other. My father was the baby of the second family. Since he had to start working for a living as a child, he seldom saw his three older half-brothers.

The idea of an excursion intrigued Uncle Alvah because my father's pastorate was then in Oklahoma City, the largest town in our state. For a country farmer, a thriving city offered far richer splendors than any small town ever could.

8

My half-uncle arrived in Oklahoma City adorned with long white whiskers, white bushy eyebrows, thick white hair, and a face that was reddened from fifty years of farming. He carried a handsome, carved cane. His blue eyes twinkled down at me as he ruffled my red-gold curls, and I fell in love immediately. He looked like a grandpa and Santa Claus all mixed together. I reached out hesitantly to touch that lovely cane, and he leaned down so that only I could hear him. "Now, honey, I don't really need this walking stick, but it sure is a handy thing to have 'case the train should have a wreck. Then I would have somethin' to knock out the windows and git free." I felt very special, for he told this just to me. I nodded my head in total agreement. I had no doubt that I would feel very secure on a journey with Uncle Alvah, and my devotion was complete.

At dinner that evening, Uncle Alvah ate three plates of food. He heaped mashed potatoes on his plate and flooded them with gravy. I could see there would be no leftovers for lunch tomorrow. He patted his round tummy after his second piece of lemon pie, thanked my mother graciously, and declared it was bedtime. My father conducted him to the Presiding Elder's room, the room always reserved for guests — the best bedroom in the parsonage. Uncle Alvah closed the door and quiet settled on the household for fifteen minutes. Then suddenly, our little parsonage rocked with a tremendous shout.

"Walter!!" roared Uncle Alvah.

I never saw my father leap from a chair so quickly, and I was right behind him. At the doorway I peered around my father's legs. There stood Uncle Alvah in his long underwear (the month was July) staring up at the electric light bulb dangling from the ceiling.

"Turn that dadburned thing off! I'm likely to do it backwards and get us all blowed to kingdom come."

I thought my nineteen-year-old brother would choke trying to stifle his laughter.

My sister, a dignified seventeen, was not so amused with Uncle Alvah. The man refused to remove his long underwear or take a bath. That underwear was on for the duration of his visit, and no one, not even my father, dared do a thing about it. The parsonage took on a funny aroma — even at seven I noticed that. I just presumed long underwear and strange smells were part of farming and accepted these facts without any trouble.

My brother took charge of Uncle Alvah for the duration of his visit, and I was allowed to tag along. I trotted adoringly beside Uncle Alvah as he gazed up at tall buildings downtown, admired our state capitol building, and inspected the meat-packing plant to discover what happened to the cattle he shipped to market. To my delight, we boarded a trolley and took him to the big amusement park at the edge of the city. There were fast, exciting rides and a swimming pool where Uncle Alvah observed his first women in bathing suits. I could hardly wait for each day to begin, just to watch and be with this wondrous relative. The final day of his visit arrived, and my brother asked our uncle what he would especially like to do.

"Well now, Herschel," he drawled, "if you don't mind, let's take your little sister out to that park so she can ride some of them rides, and maybe we kin take another peek at them wimmen in their bathing suits." There is no doubt in my mind that Uncle Alvah would have adored a modern bikini.

Off the three of us went on the trolley to the amusement park. I rode everything they would let me on, and Uncle Alvah ambled around the "swimmin' hole." After several hours we boarded a bus to return home. Neither my brother nor I thought of explaining the difference between a trolley and a bus. The bus filled immediately and drove a mile without stopping. A passenger buzzed to get off, and the driver swung the bus to the curb. Immediately Uncle Alvah jumped to his feet and yelled, "It's off the track, Herschel, it's off the track!" The whole busful of people, including the bus driver, burst into hysterical laughter. By the time he was ready to leave, everyone was calling him "Uncle Alvah" and knew that he was a farmer from Arkansas. At seven, I had observed the country come to the city. Farm life was still a vague image to me, but I was proud of Uncle Alvah — long underwear and all.

The state of Arkansas gave me my first personal experience with honest-to-goodness farm life when I was twelve. My father had purchased a new Dodge coupé with running boards and a stick shift on the floor. He thought we should give our new car a cross-country trial and attend a family reunion with Uncle Alvah and the two other half-brothers. I was ecstatic, for this was my first trip out of the state of Oklahoma, and I'd been promised driving lessons from my father. There were no laws in our part of the country about minimum driving age. My brother had been given the wheel at eight — but he was a boy.

From the middle of Oklahoma to the Ozark Mountains was a long, dusty ride, for there was little pavement in 1927. But I certainly didn't mind the rigors of the trip because my father let me drive at least half the time. My mother sat in the middle of the front seat with a hat perched on top of her head, a purse in her lap, and white gloved hands folded together. She never learned to drive and seldom spoke when the car was in motion, but we knew she loved watching the countryside whiz by at an exciting thirty-five miles an hour.

Uncle Alvah and his brothers were waiting for us on the front porch of a big rambling farmhouse when we arrived. There were dozens of hillbilly cousins and such that I had never seen before and never saw again. These rural folks possessed thick, rough hands, untamed shocks of long hair, and incredibly gentle manners. My mother's quiet ways intrigued them, and she was treated like a queen.

We stayed with Uncle Alvah for four days. At night, coal oil lamps gave off a soft glow which made flickering shadows across the ceiling. I slept in a fluffy feather bed that I could sink into up to my nose. A huge wood-burning stove filled one side of the kitchen, and breakfast included fried chicken and pie. To my chagrin, all those cousins teased me into tasting a green persimmon. My mouth felt puckered for a week. They lured me into a real swimming hole in my under-wear, but I couldn't get angry for they were all such fun. They loved having a "city" girl to tease, and I was fascinated with their ready humor and open personalities.

One evening at dusk all the men boarded a big touring car owned by one of the more prosperous brothers. My father allowed me to join the crowd. I quickly discovered what enormous fun it was to drive at top speed over a huge meadow shooting rabbits. The next morning, Uncle Alvah's wife cooked smothered rabbit and hot biscuits with gravy. That's what everyone called "eating mighty high on the hog." In the afternoon, watermelons were brought in from the fields and broken open on the front porch just so we could eat the hearts. The remainder of all that mess was thrown to the hogs. I watched in disbelief as the pigs clambered on top of each other, greedily slurping and sloshing all over those melons. The pigs made horrible noises, and I decided then and there that they were my least favorite animal.

My father was back in his element. I listened patiently while he rhapsodized about herds of cattle, flocks of sheep, and fields of grain. The afternoon of our arrival, a group from the little country church asked my father to preach a sermon. We were deep in the Ozark Mountains, and seldom did a minister pass through the area. The evening was hot, so the meeting was held under a brush arbor with torches burning at each corner. People began gathering for the service when a gang of young men suddenly raced in on horses. They circled the brush arbor several times at a full gallop, shooting guns in the air, and yelling at the top of their voices. I stood rigid with fear. Soon I noticed everyone was completely unconcerned and smiling. Even my gentle mother was unruffled. They were high-spirited young men welcoming the preacher and his family, that was all. The horses were slowed to a trot, then tethered; with greetings all around, the young men joined the service. To a shaken twelve-year-old, this was pretty exciting stuff, just like a western movie.

There was an old pump organ under a tree by the brush arbor, but no one could play this decayed instrument. My musical career had progressed to a few hymns, so my father proudly escorted me to the organ and made selections I knew, and I started pumping furiously. There were a few keys missing but the little organ had good bellows. I pulled out all the stops and played the best I could, hoping against hope that I could keep my legs working. No one seemed to notice my mistakes, so on the second hymn I had more confidence and pounded away with great glee. My father preached in cowboy boots and his best canvas hunting jacket. He was the star of the evening and loved every minute of it. And he certainly stood out among all those bushy haired men, for he had a very handsome bald head that gleamed in the flickering fire of the torches.

On our last day we walked over the land with my uncles and saw lovely rolling green hills with swirls of mist among the magnificent trees. But secretly I kept thinking about those shiny new roller skates I had received on my twelfth birthday. I was dying to get home and try out the freshly poured concrete sidewalk — a double sidewalk — that had just been laid along the main street of town. So much for the glories of the soil.

During the summer of my first pregnancy, with the Depression still threatening our lives, Gene and I needed relaxation and physical exercise. Still naive, I thought of walks in a city park or even a little tennis. But being a wife required constant compromise. After a short discussion, my husband and I climbed into our little Willis and with slow, dreary acceleration drove north out of Tulsa. Soon we were in the rich bottomland near the Verdigris River. My husband pulled off the main road onto a fairly smooth dirt road. Well, so far, so good, I thought.

Suddenly my husband turned again, into a driveway. It was less than a hundred yards to a small, white frame house set in a storybook farm. Hollywood could have shot a movie there. Big, leafy green trees stood majestically in the background. The open field next to the driveway had cute little plants all lined up in neat rows. I saw a man in bib overalls hoeing. He looked up at us and smiled and waved.

The house was small and modest, surrounded by a white picket fence. A large, sturdy-looking barn wasn't far away. Pigs rooted happily in a tidy pen, and I began to think of juicy hams and tasty bacon. There were ducks and geese about and even some little furry lambs. What a picture!

The man in the bib overalls ambled up to us. He was an elderly tenant farmer, Arvis Brotherton, who took care of the farm. He invited us in for coffee. Inside, the simplicity of the house fascinated me. The floor was made of plain boards, and I couldn't see a single throw rug. The bedstead was made of iron. The chairs were straight backed. The stove was a wood-burning model, with a long black stovepipe that cut straight up through the roof.

Arvis looked like an integral part of his surroundings. He was as clean and scrubbed as the house. He was tall and slender, always wore a straw hat, and was missing most of his teeth. Of those left, none seemed to meet. But he was kind and gentle, as are most men who work the land.

Arvis seemed to know my husband. They chatted easily while we drank coffee; then Gene eagerly left with Arvis to help with the chores. I sauntered alone over the eighty acres. Within an hour I began to revel in the rustic beauty of the place — I couldn't help it. This farm was enchanting. My husband and I drove home late that afternoon as refreshed as we had been in months.

I was more than ready for the next Sunday visit. When we arrived, Arvis Brotherton was plowing with four huge horses. My husband could hardly wait to have a turn at the plow. Only one problem marred this idyllic picture.

No bathroom was to be found within ten miles. And any way you looked at it, I was a city girl getting more pregnant by the day. The two men gravely discussed this problem out of my hearing, and that afternoon Arvis and my husband began building my very own personal outhouse. Old Arvis proudly showed me a special board he'd selected with great care. He rubbed his rough, old hands over this pretty board to show me how smooth it was — no splinters. He then announced that he was going to cut two holes in that piece of wood. I rose to the occasion and heartily approved the plan. It was quite a privilege having two men build me a personal outhouse — a two-holer.

At this happy moment, I'd almost forgotten that other farm, that windy, rocky hill east of Tulsa.

Late summer arrived hot and dusty. I pooched out like a water-melon but felt wonderful. I questioned my doctor about the feasi-bility of my continuing our Sunday outings, since he had a strong policy against long trips. Doctors were terribly strict in those days, and I wondered how they thought the pioneer women made it across the mountains and deserts. When I told him of my earlier drives out near the Verdigris, he suddenly became very angry and informed me in no uncertain terms that the first three months were the precarious times. But now, "Go ahead!" he said, glaring at me. "It's too late to take precautions. The baby's safe now." I thought that was good news, not cause for a reprimand.

The last Sunday in August, we started our usual trek in our little Willis. I was as lighthearted as ever, but my husband was unnaturally quiet. As he gripped the steering wheel, I felt a tiny cloud hovering over us. We arrived at the farm to find Arvis Brotherton surrounded by four kinfolk, including his niece. Something was drastically wrong. I could practically smell trouble in this clean, healthy air.

True to form, the men gathered with my husband and walked towards the barn where they huddled into a male circle. I joined Arvis's niece, a pleasant middle-aged woman, and we talked about cooking and my pregnancy. I wasn't the least bit interested by our usual "woman talk." I wanted to be with my husband and hear what those mysterious but friendly-looking strangers were discussing. I peeked out the window between cups of coffee. The farm was flat, so my husband was always in sight. I watched him bend down, take a handful of soil and squeeze it. Then he gently broke up the clod, examining it like a piece of jewelry. He really did like the stuff.

Even from this distance I could see that Gene was deeply moved. I glanced at the faces of the big men standing in the circle. Their smiles had disappeared. Arvis Brotherton's shoulders were sagging helplessly. I saw the grim ghost of the Depression hovering over this gentle man.

"More coffee?" beckoned the niece.

Alas, yes, one more cup, I thought.

I was burning with curiosity when the men returned from the barn, but Gene's face said, *Don't talk to me right now.* We climbed into our little coupé and slowly drove away.

"Why couldn't we stay longer?" I asked at last. "Arvis keeps the place in such perfect shape. The lambs — I saw one actually gambol, like a little child dancing."

My husband almost had tears in his eyes.

"Is something happening?" I persisted.

"Yes," he said. "This farm now belongs to the county."

"Uh . . . ." I felt a wave of morning sickness right there in the middle of the afternoon. "But how can that be?"

"The farm was part of my father's estate. It was willed to my mother along with other property in town," he explained. "Arvis can grow enough to feed himself with a little left over for trading with his neighbors. We aren't asking any rent right now. But he can't even sell enough to meet taxes."

"But what about the city property?" I wailed. "Can't you manipulate something? You're a full-fledged lawyer now."

"I tried but no banker will touch it. What little rent the city property brings in just covers mortgage payments and taxes. It's a break-even situation. My mother is lucky just to hold on to what she has. The Verdigris farm is three years behind on taxes. The banks won't loan us another penny. I can't advise my mother to take money out of the city property to save the farm. She might lose everything that way."

I felt alternately depressed and angry. I shouldn't have drunk so much of Arvis's dearly purchased coffee. Now he would have to move out to California as so many impoverished Okies were forced to do. "He seems like such a fine, solid farmer," I sighed.

"He is. Arvis owned the farm once. That's why he loves it so. He borrowed to expand and then had to let the bank take over. The bank sold the farm once and then a second time. My father acquired the property sight unseen in a three-way trade."

What complications had landed on top of hardworking farmers! None of this seemed right, and I was desperately trying to understand all these difficulties. Certainly such a tragedy for Arvis was not right, but we had all seen so much injustice. Both tenants and owners were victimized in different ways. One could only wonder which was worse, a landlord's debt or a tenant's unemployment. The Depression knew no class distinctions. We tried not to agonize over justice or injustice. We just tried to cope with the raw, not-so-pretty facts of life.

The Verdigris farm did offer me a fleeting vision. I would have moved out to those eighty acres without a moment's doubt. Such picturesque beauty had to have a certain rightness about it — at least, I thought so.

From the time we first met at the ages of fifteen and eighteen, Gene had always been sophisticated and mature beyond his years. Even for a date with me, he would arrive at our doorstep formally attired in a derby, a double-breasted gray topcoat, and spats. He seemed to enjoy my father's company at least as much as mine. Most of the time our dates ended in a chess game between my father and my future husband, while I fell asleep on the sofa.

After we were married, my husband's composure became his trademark. By contrast, I was usually excited about something. Pontifically, he would intone, "Repose is the crowning jewel in the diadem of character." That irritated the hell out of me. I simply was unable to *repose*.

I was startled early one evening, therefore, when my husband burst into our apartment yelling loudly, "Look! Just look at this check!"

I dropped everything and rushed to look at the check he was waving so triumphantly. "One thousand dollars!" I gasped. My unborn child did a back flip.

"My first real legal fee," Gene said, and I could hear the excitement and pride in his voice. "Now we can go into the chicken business and save our farm."

I was so elated that this mention of chickens saving our farm didn't faze me. For once, however, I put my foot down and insisted we drive right downtown and buy an electric refrigerator and a bassinet before our farm absorbed all that lovely money.

My husband traditionally shielded me from certain economic realities. He managed his mother's property so that she enjoyed financial security, but our own situation was always precarious. Not until years later did I learn that he had been constantly in and out of debt. He made money in an insulation business and lost it all in a zinc mine. He made money in pigs and lost it in a wheat deal. Win or lose, he was always willing to take a chance, work hard, and hope.

It was, I'm sure, a combination of masculine pride — plus the ethos of what women were supposed to be told — that kept me blissfully ignorant. All I knew was there were ups and downs, and this first big legal fee was an up.

Our new electric refrigerator was installed. It sparkled like a diamond in my dingy kitchen. Never again would I have to empty that icebox drip bowl, always overflowing and sloshing on my feet as I staggered to the sink. And never again would the awful mold and fungus of that slimy drip bowl rub off on my expanding tummy.

I was now too pregnant to worry about some distant rocky hillside. My husband disappeared out to the farm on Saturdays, but I didn't care anymore. Occasionally I heard him discussing loads of lumber, wire, fence posts, and general farm stuff over the telephone. In my ninth month, I simply put my head in the sand and tried to forget the whole thing. I was absorbed in creating a new human being.

Our first child was born with no problems, and Gene was overcome with domestic bliss. Sometimes after dinner he would unfold all the diapers, plug in the iron, and proceed to smooth out his son's pants. Where that little routine came from, heaven only knows. But I didn't interfere, for I was happy and contented.

My strength returned quickly. Our son was a few weeks old when my husband arrived from the office early. I was surprised, and secretly hoped for another thousand-dollar check.

"Our finances are now under better control," he explained carefully. "We can move into our house."

"*Our house?*" I exclaimed. "What house?"

Just before we were married, Gene mentioned some house he owned, but I was off in the clouds and paid little attention. He never referred to that piece of property again.

I listened first with bewilderment, then with undisguised irritation. He looked at me and grinned. "You see, we've never been able to afford to live in our house. I knew if I showed it to you, you'd want to live there. It's in a great location close to Woodward Park where you can take the baby for walks. Three bedrooms and a back yard with a big tree."

"And we've —"

Gene put his hand over my lips, meaning for me to shut up and listen. I didn't want another lecture, so I shut up and grinned back at him.

"We've been lucky," he explained. "The house brings in such good rent that I've been able to pay taxes and reduce the mortgage to the point where we can move in ourselves."

A house of our own! I should have been overjoyed. But I was haunted by visions of all the lumber, wire, and fence posts, costing hundreds of dollars, which had disappeared into that pile of rocks while we lived cooped up in a little apartment.

"All right," I said tersely, "when do we move?"

"This weekend." Once his mind had analyzed a problem and he came to a decision, we acted immediately. That suited me, for I enjoyed action.

I loved that house. It was solidly built, and the yard seemed spacious after apartment living. I forgave my husband. I did wonder what further secrets he might be holding back, but I was too apprehensive to ask. Somehow I knew he was being as forthright as he knew how to be. Depression economics were bizarre, and with my PK background I did not attempt to understand the causes. I only tried to cope with the results.

Happiness pervaded our home with a yard to garden, a baby to care for, and a husband to love. I thought nothing could upset me. Then my husband made a little decision that did the trick.

From my kitchen I suddenly heard rattles, squeaks, and a loud braking sound. I was afraid to look out at the driveway. Finally I summoned courage and walked outside. There stood a second-hand, red, Ford pickup truck.

"What —"

"I just made a great trade!" exclaimed my husband.

"You mean the Willis coupé is gone?"

"Forever — and good riddance. Now we can haul everything ourselves."

"I don't want to haul anything," I sighed. I walked completely around that rusting pile of junk. To me, a pickup truck was not transportation — it was a farm implement. The rest of our discussion was brief.

"What will some client think when you rattle up in that . . . contraption?"

"One of my clients has already been impressed. In fact, I'd say he was downright jealous."

End of discussion. I learned to drive a rusting farm implement.

TWO
BACK TO THE ROCK

Number two son was born. With two babies, the house and garden, cooking and friends, I heard little about our twenty-two-acre rock. I knew Gene spent a regular portion of his time there. Occasionally he brought home a few fresh eggs. I presumed this was a physical outlet for him. Some men played golf, my man played farmer. Sometimes months would go by in which nothing was mentioned about chickens, eggs, or virgin hay, and I asked no questions. The farm receded into the background of my life, but a receding image is no guarantee of a permanently disappearing vision.

One Saturday in October 1940, Gene asked me to find a baby-sitter for the next day. This was a surprise. I immediately called one of my favorite sitters and was eagerly looking forward to a day alone with my husband. He had been preoccupied with something lately. Perhaps I would find out what was on his mind.

But Gene was silent as he helped me climb up into the old red pickup. A mystical impulse seemed to guide his hands on the steering wheel. Very soon I realized we were going east through the city, heading resolutely towards the farm. We turned off the main highway on that horrible road full of chuckholes. I grabbed hold of the doorknob to steady myself, but to my amazement the dusty dirt road had been sprayed with sticky oil. The big holes were filled in with coarse gravel. "Is this the same road?" I asked.

"Yes," replied Gene happily. "The county finally came up with a few improvements. Probably auctioned off some farm for a dozen barrels of oil. The effect may not be like real asphalt but the oil does keep the dust down." Quickly he righted the truck as we skidded through the oil. Fresh oil is slippery just like mud, but I had to admit this was an improvement. We were approaching the end of the road. I became inexplicably nervous. I just did not want to be here. Then . . . .

"Telephone poles!" I screamed. "Oh no!"

Indeed, the skyline had changed. Two tiny buildings, smaller than real houses, stood atop the hill. I was given a detailed tour. One was a small shed that had been made into a chicken house. It was filthy with chicken manure and feathers. It smelled bad and looked worse, but I saw no chickens.

The other edifice was a garage with two miniature rooms and a three-quarter bath. One of the rooms held an old wood-burning cast-iron stove — shades of a Methodist parsonage! There were electric lights and, amazingly, water.

Gene stopped and looked around slowly. "A young black couple from southern Oklahoma appeared one day," he explained. "They wanted to live close to a city. The man couldn't sign his name, but he was a great worker. He and I built the chicken house and these living quarters. We raised chickens and split the cash fifty-fifty. We started small and were selling all the chickens and eggs we produced. But we couldn't expand. Just not enough buyers. The market was too small."

"Where's the black couple?" I asked.

"Gone now. They could see we weren't going to make it."

All the sunshine disappeared. I felt sad — sad for my hard-working husband and his shattered dream.

"I thought we could take one last look," sighed Gene.

One last look! I knew the pain of those words all too well. I looked out over our little piece of Oklahoma prairie. I breathed deeply, for today there was no dust whipping through the air. We had a rare windless, quiet October day — Oklahoma Indian summer at its best. The air was cool and invigorating. We started walking the property line. Down the hill we trudged, off the rocks and out across a field of virgin prairie hay. The field had turned a golden color with the autumn sun, and I happily absorbed the fresh aroma which rose up around us as our feet disturbed the grasses. A killdeer, a species of plover, ran rapidly across our path. We stepped over a small creek only a foot wide and a few inches deep. Despite the tiny flow of water, several wild flowers and scrub willows managed to grow along the creek's edge.

"We could have brought in a bulldozer and pushed up a dam for a stockpond here," Gene commented sadly.

Yes, even I could see that. The hay would have been enough for a few cows, perhaps even a horse.

"How much longer —" I started to ask.

"Two weeks. I checked at the county clerk's office the day before yesterday."

I grabbed my husband's hand as we finished our walk. We were too inured to the harshness of the times to feel any great emotion. The only solution was to be as matter-of-fact as possible, but I knew so well what all this meant to my husband. The view was so unusually clear on this exquisite day that I enjoyed walking the property line one more time. In such soft sunshine even the rocks didn't look too bad.

I was about to speak when we spotted another pickup truck parked beside ours. A tall, enormous man was waiting for us.

"Howdy," said the giant. "You Mister Gubser?"

"Sure am." I listened, amazed, as Gene acquired the faintest suggestion of an Okie drawl.

"I'm Deke. Been lookin' for you." The big man held out his mammoth paw, which engulfed my husband's hand. "I'm a driller."

As they talked, I watched this rugged, handsome man. His shoulders were thick and muscular, his hips thin, tapering into long legs. I was formally introduced. Thank goodness women were not required to shake hands, I thought. Deke's huge fingernails were lined with grease. In fact, he smelled of crude oil. In horror I watched him spit a stream of tobacco juice onto our rocky terrain.

"I do the drilling, and I got me a lease-broker. He's a lawyer type, and I oughta have him do the talking, but . . . ."

"I'm a lawyer," Gene smiled encouragingly.

"Oh." Deke eyed both of us carefully. "And this here's your land, like the man up the road said?"

"That's right," said Gene in the easiest, slickest tone of voice I had ever heard him use. What a cool customer he was all of a sudden! Something was going on here. Funny little feelings were churning around in my tummy.

"Tell you what," said Deke. "I've been driving around these parts for a couple of months now, and I figure there's oil. The way this hill comes up, real dome-like, sure makes it a likely looking place to put down a discovery well."

Our rocks had oil underneath? My head was swimming. Gene reached down and plucked a weed. His ritualistic procedure was driving me mad. Slowly he peeled off the outer husk, then stuck the stalk between his teeth. My God, I thought, all he needs is a straw hat!

"Deke," said my husband in a voice as smooth as silk, "I think you and me just might be able to work us out a deal."

Oil!? That was one product that always sold. It wasn't like chickens and eggs. You could pipe oil anywhere, even overseas, and get a big, fat royalty check every three months.

Back in 1921, when I was six, our family had moved to the small town of Duncan in southern Oklahoma. It was a typical, sleepy county seat where everyone was in bed by nine o'clock. Then a tremendous oil field was discovered on farms surrounding Duncan, and it immediately mushroomed into a complex boom town. Oil brought in a swarm of people and lots of fresh money.

My mother cautiously agreed to rent out the Presiding Elder's bedroom, after much discussion with the Missionary Society to be certain it was the correct procedure for a minister's wife to conduct such a business. On Sunday mornings, our church bulged with new people, and folding chairs had to be placed in the aisles. All this extra activity was so exciting, I stopped reading during the church service and watched the grown-ups. The ushers were having a ball seating people and handing out membership cards for them to sign. Best of all, the collection plates were piled high with green folding money. I loved giving each plate a jiggle to see if there was any silver on the bottom, even though my mother frowned at me. The ushers brought all the plates to the altar, stacked them one on top of another, then my father blessed the entire pile. A little prayer took the taint off all that money, I figured.

At night when I was tucked in bed, I could overhear my parents and neighbors discussing the tremendous influx of people — both good and bad. Women could no longer go out at night alone, whatever that meant.

Oil wells sometimes caught fire and burned for weeks. From our back porch we could see flames leaping up into the night sky. No one knew how to cap the gushers in those days, so crude oil spurted straight up into the atmosphere. Ugly oil stains regularly appeared around the white posts on our front porch. The Oklahoma wind even splattered droplets of oil on the windshield of our car, just as though raindrops were falling. One farmer had so much oil rain down on his property that the crops were ruined. He purchased another farm since that was the life he knew best, and to his dismay oil was found on his second property. He finally gave up, became a rich man and bought a large house in town. Almost everyone who had a farm around Duncan became rich. Naturally, I had visions of money suddenly gushing up out of the rocks on our farm.

Drilling for oil, however, is neither easy nor cheap. No one had put down a well in the area around our farm for over twenty years. I didn't mind if big Deke wanted to gamble his life away, and I cared even less what might happen to the slippery lease-broker after we met him. The next week, however, my husband came home and told me he was going to take out a second mortgage on our house in order to pay the taxes on those twenty-two acres. My joy vanished. When I showed resistance, my husband gave me his famous "Rabbit and Bear" lecture. This lecture can last up to two hours. The point is that a man can't kill a big bear by aiming his gun at a little bitty rabbit. "That oil pool down there under our hill is a big bear," said my husband. "We'll never find that oil if we don't spend money to drill."

"What if there isn't a pool of oil down there?" I wailed. "We could lose our house."

"Nobody said shooting at big bears was safe."

I knew it was useless to try to change my husband's mind. And, of course, he was right — it was our only hope. So far in our marriage there had always been a roof over our heads and food on the table. Ultimately there comes a time when we have to have faith. Depression years had brought many disappointments but also a surprising reserve of strength. Right now the prospect of another failure was testing the limits of my strength. I asked Gene what the geologists thought.

"I don't trust academic geologists," he said. "Deke's got more natural rock sense than a whole university full of eggheads. He's found oil where nobody has ever thought of looking."

I began scanning the want ads for small apartments.

On Friday, six days after the first talk between my husband and Deke, Gene walked into the house with a tense, highly elated air. The week had flown by in an atmosphere of crisis. Everything was arranged and the work had begun.

"We could spend the weekend at our farm," suggested Gene. "Now that we have a vacant house out there."

"You mean . . . overnight?"

"Deke will be setting up his rig. You might say all of us have a vested interest."

Vested interest? I'll say! I wasn't about to miss the beginning of our adventure. I packed food, linens, and the children into the red Ford pickup. When we arrived early Saturday morning, our desolate spread of bald prairie had been transformed into a dynamic outpost of the American oil industry. Big trucks were rumbling around, unloading complicated chunks of machinery. A tall steel mast was already poking up into the sky. Guy wires — steel cables actually —

attached to big stakes, held the mast steady. Dirty men in dirtier overalls were milling around.

Three things were strictly forbidden in an oil field — guns, booze, and women. To the roughnecks, the children simply did not exist. I bustled them and myself off to our miniature house and organized things for the weekend. The mast was erected only a hundred yards away, and I could watch the activity through a window.

Big Deke was a true John Wayne type, except that he didn't drink or curse. Like many gigantic men, his manner was mild, even gentle at times. There was so much latent power in his rugged frame that his leadership was never questioned.

I finally dared to sneak outside. I had to see the intricacies of this operation up close. Attempting to appear invisible, I sidled nearer and nearer the rig. Deke was straining against some balky piece of steel. His neck looked thicker than his head, and the veins in his forehead were bulging. A bleary-eyed roughneck, dirty and tough-looking, stood beside Deke, doing nothing.

In the kindest, easiest voice, Deke asked, "Could you budge 'er over a hair, Jake?"

Jake reacted as if he had been lashed with a bullwhip. He attacked that hunk of balking steel, willing and even eager to give himself a hernia, slip a disc, or lose a finger.

"That'll do," gasped Deke at last. The veins in his forehead subsided and disappeared. His neck returned to normal size.

I saw Jake back off and whip a flask out of his pocket for a quick nip. The rules against booze and women were now broken.

Deke's rig was a spudder. I looked at all that apparatus carefully. This spudder had a big heavy bit about eight inches in diameter and several feet long. The bit was connected to a cable which was strung up to the top of the mast. Through a system of draw works and pulleys, the bit was raised, then suddenly released. The bit would then bang down into the rock and wham a hole down, down, down to the big bear.

The actual drilling started late Saturday afternoon. The steady thump, thump, thump gave me an excited, gutsy feeling.

"How far does each thump go down?" I asked. "Two inches? Two feet?"

My husband shrugged his shoulders impatiently. Obviously this was not woman's business, but I was so curious. Why did he go to the trouble of bringing me out here? Secretly, I suspected he didn't know the answer himself.

I worked off my energy by attempting to make our tiny quarters livable. Then an idea occurred to me: why not clean up that little chicken house and make a playpen for the boys? Off I trotted with hoe in hand. I chopped and scraped at chicken manure and fought flying feathers. How did I get myself into this mess, I wondered. That night I fell into a heavy sleep but awakened suddenly at three o'clock. The children were quiet. My husband was asleep. Thump, thump, thump — it was the spudder spudding away. The crew worked twenty-four hours a day! When did Deke and his men sleep?

We began spending all our weekends at the farm, as my husband became more and more involved in the drilling of "his" well. I fixed meals in the kitchen of the little house, then puttered around doing chores. The boys were enchanted with their new surroundings and fought with each other only occasionally. One morning when I looked out the window, I was horrified to see not Deke or Jake but my *husband* perched on the very top of the mast. The month was November and the wind was freezing cold. A little rain had fallen during the night, and I could see a thin glaze of ice covering each square foot of exposed steel.

Furious and scared out of my wits, I raced out to the rig, pulling on a coat as I ran. Deke was looking up at the crown block where my husband was fiddling with the big cable pulleys.

"What . . . !" I choked. I couldn't speak. Deke quickly understood as he looked at me.

"Don't worry ma'am," he said. "He's doing real good."

"But why — ?"

"We played poker for the job," explained Deke. "Greasing the crown block is the most . . . uh . . . interesting job around here."

Interesting? I looked up again. I couldn't see a speck of safety equipment — not even a railing or a piece of rope to hang onto. I had never heard the term *macho*, but I knew exactly what had driven Gene up that mast.

"I thought my husband was a pretty good poker player," I said suspiciously.

"Oh, he is that for sure." Deke grinned slightly. "That is, when he wants to be."

I said nothing more, especially since Gene was on top of that mast. After what seemed like hours, Gene slowly began easing his way down the icy steel post. Deke's spudder was an ancient model, and the ladder was loose in places. I watched Gene's hands grabbing at the cross-beams and any other structural pieces he could get his hands on. My husband had never been a mountain climber. Athletics was not exactly his forte, although he played baseball and wrestled in high school. He was certainly not qualified to be a grease monkey on an icy oil rig.

With my heart skipping beats and my stomach churning in fear and anger, I watched him step safely onto solid ground. Then I ran and confronted him. He was taking off his gloves. I snatched the gloves away, screaming, "You'll never use these again!"

"But those are two-dollar, real leather gloves!"

"I don't care!" I turned and ran for the little house. I had embarrassed my husband in front of all those tough roughnecks, and I was glad.

I knew he was capable of fixing the truck and building a chicken house (with a little help). Okay, so he was a minor mechanic. But one look at Jake's rummy face, Deke's huge strength, and all the workers' mutilated hands convinced me I could never let my husband compete for honors in that crew. Gene followed and grabbed me in a big hug. He never said a word.

The thumping continued day after day. The men, I learned, were working in shifts. A large tractor with a blade was trucked in to dig out a mud pit right in front of the house. I watched my husband talk to the tractor "jockey" and then slip him some cash. The tractor jockey promptly rumbled down the hill and pushed up a dam for a stockpond. This told me in no uncertain terms that, for my husband, the idea of our farm was more alive than ever.

As we clattered and bumped onto our farm the following Friday, I knew something was wrong. Gene jumped out of the pickup and strode over to Deke with me not far behind. I was beginning to feel like an Indian squaw.

Deke's rugged face looked both troubled and doubtful. I listened intently, even though much of the conversation flew right over my head. Jake ambled over, and the three men stood in a tight triangle while I backed off slightly. But my vested interest — plus my ever-bubbling curiosity — kept me within hearing distance. I had to know what was going on at the rig.

"Mostly sandstone, of course," said Deke. "Some salt, but nothing to make a dome. I sure would like to see a little limestone."

Boozy Jake suddenly looked over at me and grinned. I didn't like the way he was leering at me.

"We'll take 'er down another couple of hundred feet," sighed Deke. "Looking drier than a bone, though."

To my relief, the tight triangle separated. I walked stiffly off with my husband towards our minihouse. Gene was seething with anger. "I'll kill Jake if he so much as breathes in your direction again," he muttered.

"Maybe I should stay in the house," I offered.

"This is our land," he replied. "I'm not telling you where you can and can't go. But there's no way you can hide your good looks from the roughnecks."

I drew my own conclusions. Deke was a gentleman in his way, and I liked and trusted him. Jake and the rest were dangerous riffraff who lurched from job to drink to women and back again. It dawned on me what the grown-ups were talking about back in the oil-boom days when women couldn't go out at night. I decided that only when Deke was alone with my husband would I venture near the spudder.

A depressed mood engulfed the men. They had thumped that thing down to 1,000 feet, and not a teacup of oil had appeared. Spudders are used only for shallow wells, and Deke was basing his gamble on the hope that oil was near the surface.

The accomplishment of our few weekends was one stockpond and a salty mess all over our rocks. What the heck, I thought, they'll be the county's rocks pretty soon.

The following weekend we arrived just at sunset on Friday. Deke's spudder was ominously silent. Last week's thump, thump, thump, with its mesmerizing assurance of financial security, was gone.

"We stopped dead at 1,200 feet — ran out of cable," explained Deke.

For an instant I was fearful that Gene would jump in his pickup, drive immediately to an oil-supply warehouse, and buy another thousand feet of cable at some hideous price.

Gene looked straight at Deke. "I've been walking the property for some time and stepped across my line in several spots to look at the rock outcrops. Why don't we move the spudder off the hill and punch it down again? I've got a real feeling about one particular place down there."

Deke looked apprehensive. This conversation was confusing — to me, but certainly not to the two men. Still, I didn't know if my husband was offering to sink some of his borrowed money in another dry hole (that's oil-patch talk for a well that produces no oil) or simply trying to manipulate Deke. There was money behind Deke — anyone could feel that. But whose and how much? And how free was Deke to act on his own?

"Well," said Deke, looking as though he were weighing his life's reputation, "as long as I'm here, I could go for one more time. But only a thousand feet. That last 200 feet like to wore out my spudder."

It was an awesome thing for me to watch a man like Deke come under the spell of my husband's eloquence. When we were alone, I couldn't help but ask, "You're not trying to lose Deke's money for him, are you?"

"Nope." Gene was still using his Okie drawl. "But I am trying to save our farm. Oil royalties are the only thing that will enable us to pay off the second mortgage on our house and get ahead on taxes. This next well has to be a producer."

I was not impressed. "Stop using that Okie drawl with me. What makes you think you aren't going to lose this property, Deke's money, and our home?"

"Limestone," said Gene. "Wherever there's limestone, there's a chance of finding oil. That dry hole on the hill didn't turn up a grain of limestone, but there're at least two strata running through this land. I can show you outcrops of it all over the place, and I think they're connected. I know we're going to find something with this next hole."

"The big bear?" I asked.

"Well, in a manner of speaking, yes."

I was thoroughly heartbroken. I would have settled for a couple of juicy rabbits to put in our pot.

Moving the spudder was just a messy, noisy intrusion this time. No excitement. The trash those men left behind was only a hundred yards from our minihouse. There was a huge pond of salt water and drilling mud mixed in with rocks, tin cans, tobacco juice by the gallon, and dried weeds. It looked as though someone had swirled an enormous mixer through all this repulsive glop. Our rocky hilltop was permanently scarred.

With the spudder down the hill, I tried to forget the whole thing. I needed hard labor to unwind. Fiercely, I concentrated my energies on turning the chicken house into a jungle gym for the boys. The dried chicken droppings had created a cement-like crust. The only way I could break up the mess was to flail at it with a hoe. Gray-green clouds of dust ballooned around me, covered my clothes, flew up my nose, and settled in my ears and eyes. I carried buckets of water and sloshed them over the floor until all was clean enough for my children. The boys loved that old chicken house, and there was nothing they could hurt except each other. This was a great adventure, entirely different from our little city backyard. I found boards and boxes so they could build forts and stockades. They discovered kernels of feed corn I had overlooked and proceeded to have their own banquet, much to my horror.

I toyed with the idea of planting a tree or a shrub next to the garage, but topsoil was simply nonexistent. Besides, it would take a forest to cover that mess in the front yard. Before long, I could hear the distant thump, thump, thump of the spudder. The more distance, the better, I thought.

Two weekends later, Deke was down to 950 feet. Good, I thought. Another fifty feet and this nightmare would be over.

But as Saturday wore on, an air of excitement began to build. At one point, my husband sprinted all the way from the rig up to our little house. I wondered if a man had been hurt.

"Limestone!" shouted Gene. He opened his fist to show me a few gravelly bits of whitish rock.

"And oil too?" I asked, suddenly aflame with excitement.

"No, no oil yet," he confessed. "But Deke's going down to a full 1,200 feet now. He's feeling good about it."

"But limestone — isn't that awfully common?" I asked. "Aren't gravel quarries nothing but limestone — devoid of oil?"

Gene wasn't about to be defused. He raced back down the hill. The thumping continued all Saturday night. Nothing more happened, so Sunday evening I started packing for our return to the city.

"Don't pack," Gene ordered. "We're staying."

His words had a fearful ring. Staying? For how long? Another week? A decade? I had no idea how long this oil thing could go on. "What about your law business?" I asked.

"I'm going to a neighbor's house to phone my secretary."

There was no doubt now. My husband had the fever. He became a different human being. He didn't sleep for three days and three nights. It was coffee and one game of gin rummy after another. He and the boys seemed to thrive on the excitement, but I longed to return to our real life in Tulsa.

Suddenly, Wednesday at midmorning, the thumping of the spudder stopped. The thumping of my heart took over. Exiled from the drilling activities and alone on top of that rocky hill, all I could do was wait for reports as my husband literally ran to and fro, wearing himself down to a frazzle. But he so wanted to share all this excitement with me. I peeked from the windows watching the extra activity and kept the coffeepot boiling.

"Deke's going to shoot!" announced Gene, flying past me on his way to a neighbor's phone.

Shoot? Shoot what? This time, back from the phone, Gene stopped to catch his breath. "This is the point of no return," he explained. "We're down below a layer of limestone. The bottom of the hole is right in the middle of a layer of oil-bearing sandstone. It looks to be about twelve feet thick."

"But what's this shooting?" I asked.

"We have to fracture the rock — break it up to see if oil will flow. Deke's lowering a can of nitroglycerin into the hole. He's going to set it off with a Zero Hour Time Bomb — made right here in Tulsa!"

"Well, goodie."

"Don't you understand? Zero Hour Time Bombs are manufactured right here in Tulsa and used all over the world."

I looked him straight in the eye. "Does this increase our chances of finding oil?"

"Very funny. This can be dangerous." Gene was emphatic. "They've set the bomb for one hour. This means the men must lower the nitroglycerin all the way down 1,200 feet without snagging the container. Then ten feet of sand will be poured on top of the charge. To complete the preparation, the entire hole will be filled with water to compress the explosion."

"Sounds safe enough to me," I said. "You're not thinking of greasing the crown block during this procedure, are you?"

"That doesn't merit an answer."

Suddenly an earthquake shook the ground. I watched, completely dumbfounded as a thousand feet of water shot straight up into the sky. I thought they were only trying to break up some rock way down in the hole. "Looks like they overdid it," I finally managed to gasp.

"Not these guys." Then Gene was off running down the hill.

"But what now?" I screamed after him.

No answer. I was left in the lurch. The agony of enforced ignorance was more than I could bear. I threw warm clothes on the boys, shoved them into the chicken house, and raced down the hill. Not even Jake and his sots-in-arms could scare me off now.

My husband was with Deke. The crew was standing around the hole. It was full of dirty water. The water, I noticed, was bubbling and flowing out of the hole. Then, all of a sudden, the dirty brown water turned very black.

"Oil!" shouted Deke. It was a free-flowing well — not an old-fashioned gusher, but oil was running all over the place. "We gotta plug it!" roared Deke.

The crew quickly lowered an expandable plug into the hole. Then I watched Deke swagger up to Jake, roughly grab a half-pint bottle out of his grimy overalls pocket, and take a long pull — the first and last time I ever saw Deke take a drink.

I felt enormously relieved for this rugged man. He had been persuaded by my silver-tongued husband to take a final risk and now his reputation as "the driller with the magic touch" was more secure than ever.

My husband gave me a tremendous big-bear hug and kiss. "Merry Christmas," he said. Instantly I forgave him for his foolhardy zeal and for the hectic days and nights of oil fever.

"Are we . . . rich?" I asked cautiously.

"I doubt it," he laughed. He was a risk-taker, but still a realist.

Gene fell into bed before lunch and slept for nineteen hours. The next day, Thursday, a newspaper reporter drove out to interview us, and suddenly we were in the news. The publicity was an unexpected boost for Gene's legal business. Since an attorney couldn't advertise, the oil story gave him some publicity which helped bring in several clients.

That was all just lovely and exciting, but what I was interested in were those *royalty checks*. I had mentally spent that money several times over. Now I really started thinking of redecorating our house in town and buying myself some new clothes.

But first we had to convert that syrupy black stuff into money. As long as the big bear was hibernating down deep in his cozy little cave, he was merely an obscure part of the local geology. Even though I had been around oil wells most of my life, I had no idea of the intricate problems of actually producing and getting rid of all that unrefined crude oil. Deke brought in a 5,000-gallon tank on the back of a flatbed truck. He deposited the tank on our rock, and the oil filled it up to the brim. Deke found another tank, and the well happily gurgled out more black gold.

A trucker with a portable tank drove to our farm and hauled off load after load of oil. My husband found the nearest pipeline company, which had a branch line a few miles away. At first, just for one well, the company could not justify laying a pipeline all the way to our property.

But Deke was now a busy man. Ours was the first successful well out of about fifty Deke and others drilled in the "Airport Pool," as our area, two miles from the Tulsa airport, came to be called. Even though the wells were shallow and did not produce for very long, the newspaper accounts recalled the first big oil strikes in the Tulsa area

— the Glenn Pool and Burbank strikes — which had made Tulsa the "Oil Capital of the World." Many people drove out to the airport just to watch all the exciting activity of drilling an oil well.

As more wells began producing, the pipeline company was more than happy to stretch out its branch line to take our oil. Now we were stuck with a dirty, old oil tank on our property. Both the oil tank and Deke were to reappear some time later as very important parts of our farm — and in no way connected with oil.

The Airport Pool was shallow, and the area was soon overdrilled. Our well produced for only two years. Though short-lived, those royalties were crucial for us. The oil money enabled us to pay off the second mortgage on our house in town and put us ahead on property taxes for both the twenty-two-acre farm and our house. Our actual style of living remained unchanged; it was still hand-to-mouth for groceries, utilities, bandages, and toys for the boys. As far as I was concerned, the government was sucking up all our money. Somewhere in this whirl, I felt I deserved some new clothes. I was tired of looking like plain old Mary Redneck, with a scarf tied around my hair as I sloshed around in all that muck, wearing boots and rough pants.

That singular thought plagued me all one weekend, which of course was spent on our farm. Except for two dry holes and one producer, our land was still essentially unchanged bald prairie. I couldn't honestly share Gene's pride in his unused stockpond which had slowly filled with water, tadpoles, and fish.

I did have to admit there were glorious, soft days when walking over our twenty-two acres was almost a joy. Oklahoma has lots and lots of sun. The sky is big, and the sunsets are among the world's most beautiful sights. The dust and wind often settle in the evenings, creating a real sense of stillness and peace. I watched the mother quail guard their precious eggs. When the babies were hatched, I worried over their lack of protection from coyotes and stray dogs. I loved to see a covey rise from the field with a great whirring of wings. But I was just a city girl on a weekend trip to an arid piece of rural Oklahoma that had captivated my husband.

An old fence bordered our property, and on rare occasions neighbors would appear. Gene always managed to get into prolonged conversations with these real farmers. One Sunday afternoon I listened vaguely while Gene and a neighbor talked over the weather, oil prices, and the dryness of the soil. I was carefully looking for more birds when I overheard some mention of property values. I began to pay attention.

"Oh, I reckon as how $100 an acre is about the going price," observed the neighbor. "I'd sure sell for that."

"So this eighteen-acre parcel here, that fits into my property, you'd take $1,800 even for it?" Gene had reverted to his Okie way of talking. I was too dumbfounded to speak up.

"Well, it's been passed over by the drilling," said our neighbor. "The grazing hasn't been too good. You say you've got a mind to buy?"

My husband pulled a checkbook out of his pocket and wrote a check for $1,800. I was choking with anger, but I had been too thoroughly trained to interfere. I'd roast in hell before interrupting two menfolk negotiating a business deal.

My husband held out the check across the barbed wire fence. "The money's in the bank," said my husband in his most incontestably assuring legal manner.

"Why . . . I think I'm going to shake on this," said our neighbor, grinning from ear to ear. The two men firmly shook hands. The deal was now absolutely irrevocable.

The split second we were out of earshot I exploded. "How can you possibly justify . . . !" I went on for several minutes.

Finally, after biding his time, my husband said, "Twenty-two acres is an odd-sized plot. Now we've got forty acres, an even sixteenth of a section. And besides, these eighteen acres are all in pure virgin prairie hay. Not costly at all."

"Virgin prairie hay? Why all this emphasis on virginity? I can't see how it makes the slightest iota of difference," I protested bitterly.

"Oh, you will," said my husband. "You see, we're going to live here."

Eighteen more of those windy acres! I thought he was losing his mind. I wanted some new clothes, not more acres. Oh well, I had a beautiful pair of Justin boots and two pairs of Pendleton pants. I could see myself wearing that ensemble for the rest of my life, while raising nothing but a passle of boys. We were land barons now, all right. Our farm had a garage, a couple of lean-to rooms, a chicken house, and an old oil tank. Some estate!

The following day I found a baby-sitter. I drove straight downtown and bought three dresses, two skirts, four blouses, a pair of shoes, and silk hose. I *charged* everything. By the time I got home, my anger was gone, and I was filled with remorse. I hid all my purchases and waited anxiously for the bills to arrive in the mail.

The day of reckoning came.

"I haven't seen you wearing anything new," said my husband.

I rushed to our bedroom, reached in the back of the closet, pulled out my prettiest new dress, and hurriedly changed.

When I reappeared he smiled broadly. "You look great! Why don't we go out for dinner?"

I breathed an immense sigh of relief. Maybe I was second to some distant piece of land, but at least I counted. It was nice being in love, even in the Depression.

THREE

THE LITTLE
RED HUSSY

By 1940, our oil well was down to a dribble, and the quarterly royalty checks were too small to buy a sack of groceries. We were still living from week to week as most couples did in those times, for the Depression was still with us. There was no way my husband could suggest moving out to the country.

Our farm, with the junky little buildings and the dwindling oil activity, had taken on a faint personality and aroma. The air smelled of oil, virgin prairie hay, and dust. I'd seen, if not met, a couple of our neighbors. We went there two or three weekends a month now. The drive was just over six miles, and gasoline was cheap.

By this time I had developed some vague notion of the seasons of an Oklahoma farm and how important they were. Summer: hot and dry. Winter: cold and dry. Spring: windy all the time, with sudden torrential rainstorms and a few tornadoes roaring through. Autumn: two delightfully pleasant weeks every year.

When it came to fauna and flora, I was a little shaky. I could recognize prairie hay — that's tall grass. Sparrows and meadowlarks and hawks are easy to identify. We had turtles that I was supposed to call "land terrapins." My real expertise, however, was in recognizing all our sandstone as sandstone. No problem there!

Our stockpond was at last full of water and about fifty feet across. But the water was muddy and murky. Once I saw a small snake slither into the pond, and that made me uneasy. My husband's favorite Sunday afternoon occupation was sitting on the dam throwing rocks into the water. He could skip a flat rock seven or eight times. The boys loved imitating him. They relished poking around the water's edge and fell in only once a month or so.

Deke was now in charge of servicing the wells of the Airport Pool. He decided to give up drilling for he had turned thirty recently and considered himself an old man. My husband and I, now in our mid-twenties, were undecided about the old man bit, but we knew Deke was edging toward settling down.

We were walking up the hill one Saturday afternoon, with the boys kicking rocks at every step, when Deke chugged onto the farm in his pickup. To our amazement he had a woman with him. Bashfully he made the introductions — her name was Floss. True to form, my husband drifted off with Deke. Having been raised as a PK, I was used to entertaining all kinds of people, so I took Floss inside to brew a fresh pot of coffee.

Floss had very little to say. Her delicate little face had a bluish tinge through the pale skin. She was frail and thin. I figured she had had tuberculosis sometime. I shoved the boys outside into the fresh air.

About the only thing I could get out of Floss was that she thought "Deke is the finest man that ever there was." We all liked and admired Deke, I told her. I chattered away about the farm and the oil wells and carefully looked at her. I kept wondering what this huge man could see in this poor, little, consumptive creature.

I glanced out the window. Deke and my husband were shaking hands, so I knew another deal had been made. I just hoped we hadn't bought another forty acres.

The moment Gene and I were alone, I asked, "Are Deke and Floss married? She wasn't wearing a ring."

"I didn't ask," said Gene.

"Where'd he meet her?"

"First Street."

I was horrified and titillated. First Street was Tulsa's red-light district. I considered it the height of daring to drive down First Street at noonday in the middle of the week in a locked car with my husband at the wheel. Somehow poor, consumptive Floss didn't fit my image of a hooker.

Big, rugged Deke was an unusual man. Despite his rough appearance, he had a wonderfully compassionate streak in him. I have seen him stop his truck, pick up a wounded dog, bind its broken leg, and gently nurse the animal back to health. He was from northeastern Oklahoma close to Ozark country. Between oil-well jobs he drove back home to see a brother who was crippled and in a wheelchair. He adored this brother and always made certain he was comfortable and had money for food.

Deke was entering a new phase of his life, and it looked as though he wanted to settle down with Floss and take care of her. He made good money tending the Airport Pool but had no decent place to live close to his work. Gene made a deal with Deke. The couple could live rent-free on our farm. In return, over the next couple of years, Deke and my husband would add another room on the minihouse, repair the chicken house, and start raising chickens and eggs again. They decided to add a pigpen and perhaps build a shed for a milk cow or two. Deke would receive half the profits. We would wind up with the improvements plus the other half of the income.

Amazingly, I became quite interested and even elated. Our rock hill would become a real farm — a place we could visit on weekends to work, relax, and see animals producing. Our growing children could have exposure to something more than a murky, unused stockpond.

Deke and Gene worked well together. There was an interesting bond between this huge roustabout and my gentle husband. I watched one Sunday as they were working on the slanting roof of a small cowshed. Gene accidentally slammed his hammer full force on his left forefinger. He slowly laid the hammer down, looked at his bleeding hand, but instead of the expected flood of gutter profanity, he said, "Oh, pshaw." Deke couldn't believe his hardened ears. He laughed so hard he almost fell off the roof.

Our minihouse grew, and the couple moved in. More fencing was installed, and soon we had a cow and three pigs (still my least favorite animal). Deke trucked in chicken feed and purchased chickens, which soon began laying. Then lo and behold, Deke brought in a machine and cut all that virgin prairie hay for the very first time. I never could see the difference after those plants lost their virginity. We wound up with twenty tons of hay. Deke, Gene, and I scrubbed out that old oil tank and stored the hay in it. The tank made a dandy hay barn, except for the faint aroma of crude oil that we could never get rid of.

What a thrill for my husband — we now owned an authentic working farm!

I was lukewarm about the whole idea, but I could see the benefits. My husband had everything working as planned, even though there was no way those forty acres could support a family. Our grocery bill decreased; after each weekend visit we carried milk, eggs, cream, and a couple of dressed chickens back to the city. Even frail little Floss gained a hint of color in her cheeks. All this activity was a wonderful substitute for golf or tennis.

Each improvement permitted a new venture. As each venture panned out, we could move forward into new developments. There seemed to be no end to what could be accomplished on those forty acres. My husband began talking about sheep and horses and geese and even, for God's sake, peacocks. The feathers, he claimed, were worth a fortune.

I naively presumed that our goal of a real, operating farm had been reached, and that this pleasant and profitable weekend diversion might go on for years and years.

Pearl Harbor smashed into our world. Within a few days, a thousand things changed.

Before his drilling days, Deke had spent several years in the Navy. With his prior military experience, he was drafted immediately after Pearl Harbor. Both Deke and Floss disappeared from our lives. We never saw or heard from either of them again.

We were left alone with a producing farm. A farm needs a pair of hands seven days a week, not just on weekends. We tried to recruit somebody — anybody — to run the place. Everyones' lives had changed, and most people, women included, were going into factories or the military.

"That's it," announced my husband. "We're moving to our farm ourselves. We'll eat better and live better. We cannot allow that land to go fallow. It's now or never."

Strangely enough, I couldn't disagree. There was talk of rationing. In town we might have to make do with less than what we could have if we lived on the farm and grew our own food. Besides, I had become more and more involved with those forty acres of northeastern Oklahoma prairie. It had become fun to kick at those rocks, pull at the strong weeds, and walk through the tall grasses. The land was ours free and clear, and that was a good feeling. As a child, I was accustomed to moving and starting a new life every few years. Perhaps the time had arrived when I should say good-bye to our city home.

The building of the house on the farm before Pearl Harbor had been a gradual process. With the work Deke and my husband had completed, you could say there was a kitchen, two bedrooms, and a garage. To make a real home for the family we had become, we needed a living room, a porch, and maybe another bedroom. My husband and Deke had dug out the foundation for these new additions by hand and had even poured the concrete. But that's as far as the available money would go.

Gene's plan now was to borrow enough to finish our farm house. Given our slightly improved situation, he figured that shouldn't prove too difficult. Gene was so certain all would go well that he suggested I accompany him to the bank. That would certainly be a new experience for me, so I dressed in my best suit and topped myself off with a perky hat. In grand style, we drove to the Second National Bank in our rusting red pickup.

I was formally introduced to Mr. Zanis, a loan officer. I sank down into a luscious leather chair to watch the happy show unroll. Gene had a small folder with drawings and financial statements and other mysterious documents I had never seen. I was so proud of him as he

43

presented his case in his usual smooth, professional manner. Mr. Zanis leafed through the folder carefully. He seemed to be nodding approval. The fact that our house was half built impressed him. My husband's financial statement showed promise.

Then Mr. Zanis came to the final sheet of paper. His face turned gray. "Mr. Gubser . . . Mrs. Gubser . . . ." His voice sounded acutely embarrassed. "I'm afraid I can't . . . uh . . . approve this loan."

My husband looked insulted. I jerked straight up in my perky little hat.

"Could I ask why?" asked Gene with strained politeness.

"This projected house is not in the city. It's nonurban. It's . . . *rural*."

Those words were spoken with the resounding voice of doom. "Nonurban" and "rural" came out as if Lucifer himself were consigning the entire project to the eternal fires of hell.

"And what's wrong with that?" asked my husband. "I own the land free and clear. I'm paid up on taxes. The garage and three rooms and even the foundation are debt-free. Our city house shows considerable equity. My income is respectable, if not dramatic. The farm is more than breaking even. Why — ?"

"The problem is the women," sighed Mr. Zanis. "Your finances are exemplary. If the house were in the city, I would personally guarantee approval of this loan today. But we've had a miserable record with rural loans. The women can't take it. Isolated out on some godforsaken patch of rural property, they turn to drink. Sometimes they abandon their husbands and even their children. I personally know two women who went stark raving mad. They had to be carried off to the funny farm — if you will excuse the expression."

"But —" I started to protest. I could almost see horns growing through Mr. Zanis's perfectly combed hair as he continued lecturing me. I sighed. Another sermon.

"It's the wind," he said. "You'll hear it howl around the corners of the house. You will hear wolves — *see* wolves. How do you think the legend of the werewolf got started? By lonely women out on the farm, isolated from the comforts of city life — the only life that is

44

fully human. Even if you do obtain financing from another source, *please* consider the fate of those who have gone before you."

We walked out of the bank in shock. I was confused and frightened. Mr. Zanis had been deadly serious. He had seen the results — if not in person, at least in the history of foreclosures. Mr. Zanis had succeeded in putting some serious doubts in my mind. I wanted to be on our farm — not a funny farm.

But my husband was soon laughing. "Never mind," he said blithely. "I'll find another bank. One that hasn't had to foreclose on farmhouses. Perhaps one that hasn't even made any farm loans."

"But what about all those reasons for foreclosure? The drink and, my God, the insanity?"

"That's no problem," assured my husband as he hugged me. "First, we will make sure you always have a car in first-class running condition. Second, I'll be around a lot. And third, you're you."

Gene always had a gift for making convincing arguments. Sure enough, before too long he found a savings and loan willing to advance us the money. After my first real experience with bankers, I was anxious to prove Mr. Zanis completely wrong. Werewolves, indeed.

Now we were ready to push on and finish the house. With cash in the bank, Gene drove to the lumberyard with a long list of materials. He walked up to the counter with a happy smile and showed the clerk a list of building supplies.

"Sorry," said the clerk. "Everything's frozen. It's the war."

Government bureaucracy had invaded our personal lives. How ironic! Now that I was all set to go back to the soil, I was stuck in the city. During the last few months, I had fed and watered chickens, collected and cleaned eggs, thrown garbage at the pigs, watched Gene milk a cow — even tried it myself, with some success. I was fascinated with the softness and pliability of a cow's udder and the wonderfully earthy aroma in a closed cow shed. I was finally looking forward to farm life, despite the haunting words of Mr. Zanis. But until this government freeze was over, there would be no farm for me at all.

My husband was even more frustrated. He told me he could see stacks and stacks of lumber right there in the lumberyard, and the mill wanted to sell — they were seriously overstocked.

Blood pressure elevated, Gene charged into a new government office in the downtown Federal building. He demanded to see the regulations. He read every word with his rattrap mind tightly set. Somewhere in all those prepositions and adverbs there must be a loophole.

Snap! By adroitly combining the intentionally vague meanings of several isolated paragraphs, Gene proved to the bureaucrats that because he had already poured the foundation, he was entitled to finish our house. Ours was a victory for the individual, and my loyalties have never wavered.

At last the big living room began to take shape. We had a delightful time planning every corner of that long room with a beamed ceiling, wide oak-plank flooring, and a massive fireplace. A screened porch completed the building — a necessity during Oklahoma summers in those non-air-conditioned days.

As we planned and built, our happiness was overshadowed by the war and the draft which hovered over us and all our friends. I could recognize the soldier in a man like Deke, but not in my husband. Deke could take a score of men and shout, "Charge the bunker!" My husband would say, "Gentlemen, I see a bunker, quite poorly constructed, but occupied by several Oriental-looking persons who are armed with machine guns and one small bazooka. I do not believe the bazooka is in operating condition. Now, I would like to hear the pros and cons . . . ."

All of us who had small children dreaded the idea of fathers being marched off to war. I had to admit this was a selfish feeling amid all the patriotic rhetoric flooding the nation. I knew Gene was making his own evaluations. We talked it over. "I'll try for the FBI," he said. "They're screaming for lawyers."

He filled out an application and drove to Oklahoma City for an interview. He returned in a thoughtful mood. "They would like me to join the FBI, but an older man on the board told me to withdraw my application because I have two small children. The FBI moves its people all over the country, he said, and it would be difficult for you and the children to move with me. His opinion is that the United States will win the war on the factory floor. We must swarm over the Pacific with airplanes and glut Europe with tanks."

This was my first exposure to high military strategy. "So, what did he suggest?"

"He felt that with my business and legal background, I would be more benefit to my country if I worked for a factory and helped outproduce the enemy."

"Sounds great. But what factory?"

"There's an aircraft factory near the airport, about two miles from our farm. I'll check it out first thing tomorrow."

Our farm home was almost finished. The walls were of knotty pine, and the fireplace of native Oklahoma stone. I even had a desk built into one corner with a cubbyhole for my typewriter — a big upright model I'd picked up secondhand for twelve dollars. At the opposite end of the room was a huge breakfront to hold my dishes and silverware — all in drawers and on shelves. I didn't have to save boxes for the next move — and the move after that. This was exactly the home I wanted. Now all I needed was a husband.

Gene did go to the Spartan Aircraft factory. During the 1930s, Spartan manufactured a sleek, small airplane in competition with Cessna and Beech. With the country plunged into war, Spartan was churning out parts for military planes. Gene was grabbed immediately as a priority clerk by the purchasing department where he began to do battle with the enemy — which turned out to be red tape.

Commuting from Tulsa took almost an hour each way, since traffic was increasing with the wartime expansion of all forms of manufacturing. In two more months, however, we would be living on the farm within ten minutes of the factory. Food rationing loomed before us, but we began to view our new life in idyllic terms. We would be making a significant contribution to the war and still be able to give our children a healthy, decent life.

Then, suddenly, my husband quit his job. I was appalled. "Why?" I asked over and over. I knew the Army would draft him any day, and I would be left holding the bag.

Finally my husband explained. He was very disturbed over the way the purchasing department was being run. Certain persons at the factory were overly eager to stockpile critical materials and were technically breaking the law in doing so. My husband was afraid he was being set up as the fall guy. He wanted out before the ax fell on him.

I was petrified. Here we were on the verge of a full-scale war, and my husband was now liable to be drafted. What would I do with a dusty farm — isolated and alone — with two young boys and all those quirky dumb animals?

"Can't you protest or write a letter or something?" I asked in desperation.

"Maybe. Probably won't amount to much," he grumbled.

But my husband did write a letter as I looked on anxiously. It was a long, detailed, legal-sounding letter. He mailed it off, and I counted the hours of each passing day.

A phone call came. A man asked to speak to my husband. The man gave his name, which at the time meant nothing to either of us. The man's name was J. Paul Getty.

I never got to know Getty. My husband didn't tell many stories. But here and there a few nuggets got out. Before the war, Getty was apparently only vaguely aware of the fact that he owned Spartan Aircraft Company. When the war broke out, Getty went to Washington. He fancied himself as quite a yachtsman and offered himself to the Navy as a commander of ships. This seemed logical enough since he owned a yacht or two that had been commandeered for military use. The Secretary of the Navy, however, had other ideas. He told Getty that he could do more for the war effort if he'd go to Tulsa and straighten out Spartan Aircraft Company.

Getty, in several prewar financial maneuvers, had attempted to gain control of one particular oil company by buying another. Spartan merely happened to be owned by yet another oil company that wound up in Getty's hands as a result of these maneuvers. The Secretary of the Navy, however, was acutely aware of Spartan and of what America's role in aviation would mean in the war. He finally managed to impress Getty with the contribution Spartan could make. Getty spent most of the war in Tulsa making that contribution.

Getty was so impressed with my husband's letter that he asked for a follow-up interview. Gene was rehired on the spot to straighten out the purchasing department. Soon after completing that assignment, Gene became manager of materials. By the end of the war he was the factory manager, second only to Getty. This may sound impressive, especially in retrospect, but from my view as a wife, a mother, and a woman stuck on a farm, I was married to an absentee husband. Sixty-hour weeks were normal, eighty-hour weeks were not unusual, and sudden trips out of town that lasted days and days were standard operating procedure.

But I enjoyed one little fantasy. I knew the name Krupp from my college history of World War I. It was Krupp and his factories against Getty, my husband, and Spartan Aircraft. I heard enough about Getty to know that he was exceptionally gifted as a businessman. An efficient realism permeated his approach to all problems. Nobody was hired or fired because of his pedigree, social connections, or other extraneous factors. Everything was based on ability. The outcome of the war seemed inevitable to me. I wondered why Japan ever bothered to attack. I knew the Japs and the Krupps were fools to take on Getty and my husband. Now we just had to show them.

Before I knew what my husband's new job meant in terms of life on the farm, we were approaching moving day. I grew more excited. The prospect of actually moving to the country was more thrilling than bringing in an oil well.

Once the decision to move was made, I was ready for action. After all the lectures, the philosophical discussions, our short oil experience, the many disappointments, and the constant pushing and pulling by unexpected circumstances including a world war, I could hardly believe we were packing our possessions for our move back to the soil. All our friends were aware of what we were doing. Few could understand why. My bridge club friend Polly Heddlestone was especially intrigued.

Polly and Frank Heddlestone were in their second pregnancy. She was so funny about childbearing and child raising that her constant chatter never bored me. Polly wore her hair swept high in an elaborate coiffure, chose the latest fashions in garbled profusion, and constantly experimented with weird eye makeup. Frank had majored in political science and obtained a master's degree in business administration. He was a tall, charming man whose conversation was always knowledgeable and stimulating on any subject. Polly, by contrast, had just barely made it through high school and was now compulsively reading the Harvard Classics in a desperate effort to keep up with her bright young husband. I could tell exactly what volume she was reading by her conversation. They were fascinating friends and a marvelous study in complete contrast. Their Depression experiences had been similar to ours. Frank was an insurance man who was slowly recouping every penny his father had lost in the early thirties. He glowed with easy confidence and an urbane social manner.

To Polly, our move seemed puzzling, and she expressed doubtful curiosity about our reasoning. But I felt she was a devoted friend, despite her difficulty in understanding our personal goals. Polly had even begun to show a slight hint of jealousy as we became more involved with our farm. "Oh, you really are weekend lady and gentleman farmers!" she would say. She had never seen our bleak, rocky hillside — until moving day.

We began our final packing Friday afternoon. Our house was rented with the tenant scheduled to move in on the following Monday. Polly and Frank showed up early Saturday morning to help us move. I looked at Polly's printed skirt and yellow, high-heeled sandals and pictured her trying to climb over our rocks. But she and Frank dutifully carried boxes, lamps, and chairs out to the red pickup. Their trunk and back seat were soon filled with books, clothes, and rugs.

Gene was delighted to have Frank's strong back to assist in moving the heavier items. He was extremely fond of Frank but couldn't stand Polly's never-ending chatter. Warily I watched the agitation showing on his face.

"Be nice!" I hissed as we crisscrossed paths. "They're really help-ing." Gene groaned but said nothing. His face was grim with deter-mination. He was willing to accept free labor regardless of the cost.

In caravan style we led the way in what Polly called our "cute little red truck." As we rattled towards the farm, Gene looked at me, smiled, and said, "Only two more days and we'll never have to make this trip again." I had a warm feeling in my tummy.

When our caravan rolled to a stop in front of our newly completed home, Frank jumped out of his car to join Gene and me. He said absolutely nothing — he just looked. There was a slight awkward-ness, which was not like Frank. I began looking at all we owned through his eyes. He stared down the hill at our ugly little oil well. He looked over at the small chicken house and rickety cowshed. He glanced with slight amazement at our oil tank, which I'm sure he could smell from where we were standing. There was not a tree or shrub to soften the house or the view. And then, there was the front yard — still a slush pit. A slush pit is oil-patch talk for a filthy, sloppy quagmire where old oil and grease, spilled during drilling, are mixed in with rocks, discarded chunks of rusty steel, dirt, boards, and brine. A dry hole often produces brine — very salty water — instead of oil. Nobody wants the brine, so it's left in the slush pit while the drillers rush to the next well in search of their precious black gold.

"What a . . . neat place," he said at last. By the tone of his voice I knew he was trying desperately to mean what he said. I hugged Frank and turned back to find Polly.

Polly was still in the sedan. Frank and Gene pulled a sofa from the back of the pickup and started toward the house. Then and only then did Polly emerge from her car. She ran to me in tears and clutched me tightly. "Oh, you poor, poor dear! You can't be serious. Out here, in this desert?"

I tried to laugh and put her at ease, but Polly was distraught. "You'll die!" she blubbered. "Your skin will dry out. You'll get horrible huge muscles doing the heavy chores. And think of the messy clothes you'll have to wear all the time. Please, for your sake — and mine — come back to the city."

"It's a little late now," I said, sobered by the intensity of her outpouring. "Besides, I won't be doing all those chores." Nevertheless, I could hear a faint echo of banker-priest Zanis's voice. Why was everyone so afraid of life just outside the city? We weren't that far out. I still planned to shop in town — every other day if necessary. But I knew Polly was sincere in her reaction and that she would never really grasp our feelings about the soil.

"We do have neighbors," I volunteered at last, trying to reassure and cheer my friend.

"Where?" she demanded tearfully.

"You can't see them from here. You have to drive back a ways." Heavens, I was beginning to talk like an Okie farmer!

I watched a transformation wash over Polly. She could see we were in earnest. Frank and Gene were down to the lamps now. I felt Polly beginning to look at me in a new, slightly condescending light. She was busily dabbing at her painted eyelids, trying not to smear her perfectly applied makeup.

"Well," she concluded, "better you than us."

Suddenly Polly felt too pregnant to help anymore. "What if I needed a doctor right away?" she asked. Frank and Polly left as soon as our possessions were unloaded. My husband snorted as they drove off, but I felt a little sad.

Gene put his arm around my shoulders and said, "I have a little surprise for you. Sort of a welcome-back-to-the-soil present."

I smiled. What woman can be unhappy over a present?

"I've found a car for you," he said proudly.

"A car all my very own? Not a truck — a real car?" I couldn't believe such good fortune.

"Our filling-station man in town came into my office the other day and offered his 1936 Ford for $350. He couldn't make any more payments so he wondered if I wanted the car. I grabbed his offer before he could sit down. The two of us will pick up your car Monday."

That little black car took me all the way through World War II. By the time we were ready to sell the little jewel, there was a hole in the floorboard — I could actually see the pavement as I whizzed around town running errands. It also inhaled a quart of oil with every other tank of gas. But the motor never needed any attention. We sold my car in 1946 for $500. They just don't make them like they used to!

Within a week we were settled. Gene had only a ten-minute drive to work, but with the lengthening hours of his job I saw him less and less. He was up at five o'clock each morning to milk two cows. In the evening he had to milk the cows again, feed the pigs, and perform other chores I knew little about. Gene was constantly thinking of ideas for improving our little patch of oil-stained rocky turf. At the end of the first week, he stated, "We need a tractor. That's agriculture, and I'll bet tractors aren't frozen yet."

I had just walked in from the kitchen. "That's fine," I said. "But first we need water."

"Water?"

"It's not running anymore. See for yourself."

"Call Willy Wilson. He knows all about our water line." My husband hugged and kissed me heartily, patted my cheek and said, "I've got a war to fight. *You* take care of it." And off he roared to the factory.

At least I still had a husband to kiss me good-bye, I thought with a shrug. I looked at the single bottle of water we had left and groaned. We were settled on our farm just one week, and the first big problem had burst on us unexpectedly.

"You take care of it," echoing in my ears, had an alarming sound. Suddenly I had the feeling this was the way I would fight the war. I would have to run the household *and* this rocky farm with all its animals waiting to be fed. The words of my father's sermon came back to me: "Gird your loins and get the job done."

I braced myself, shook my head, and telephoned Willy Wilson. To my great relief his gravelly, brusque voice said he'd be right over.

Two years before, this same Mr. Wilson had helped my husband lay pipe for water. Apparently Wilson was a man of all trades, and among those was a part-time plumber. Now that the water had stopped running, he was the natural person to find the problem.

I wandered outside to wait for him in what I now considered my front yard. What an unholy mess! There was not a blade of grass. In the center were the remains of our dry hole. Deke and his crew had left a huge hole that reminded me of an abandoned coal-mining strip pit. Right next to the hole was the slush pit.

Not the tiniest weed or sprig of grass could grow within yards of the slush pit because of the brine. The dirt was literally bleached white. At times this pit was bone dry, then it would turn wet and gooey for no apparent reason. I wanted to stick a sign in the middle — *Danger, Keep Out!* — but I feared the sign would disappear right down into the hole, along with my sons.

I was blessed with an imagination and could envision all this covered with green grass. I had a secret plan that could be quite simple. First I would wash all the brine out of the pit with a hose. Then when we received the new big tractor my husband planned to order, I would have him plow and disk and rake until the dry hole and the slush pit were no more. The boys would adore playing croquet on a velvety lawn. I thought my plan shouldn't take more than two or three weeks once we had water and that new tractor.

I strolled around the slush pit indulging in this lovely reverie until I spied Willy Wilson walking from the road onto our property. Willy Wilson was an older man, already half bald. He was short, about five foot six or so, and he must have weighed around 220 pounds. He rolled from side to side as he walked. A big, soggy, unlit cigar protruded from his mouth. He spit every so often as he waddled. His hands were short, broad, and dirty.

But I knew as a preacher's daughter to check his eyes. If they were bleary and bloodshot I was in for bad trouble. Willy Wilson's eyes were clear as glass. The man was not a heavy drinker.

"Our water — "

"I know," he grunted. He looked at our slush pit. "Salt's got your pipe. Rusted clean through, I betcha."

"What do you suggest?" I asked.

Wilson looked at me with patient male resignation. "I don't suggest nothin', ma'am. What I'm gonna do is dig up the pipe all the way through this slush pit, put in brand-new galvanized pipe if I can find any, then wrap it up good in tar paper."

"Oh," I said respectfully. Then I watched Wilson go to work. The pit was about forty feet in diameter. He started near the leak with a hand shovel. How could a man his age dig a forty-foot trench with a hand shovel, I wondered. But then, I was just beginning to know Willy Wilson.

When lunchtime arrived I carried out an enormous plate of food. I had watched Wilson dig at that ditch with a slow but very powerful rhythm. He ate his lunch the same way. When he was down to the last few scraps, he showed no sign of slowing. I rushed back to my kitchen and piled food onto a second plate. Obviously I would have to cook another dinner for my family.

Wilson was waiting patiently. He took the second plate without a word and attacked it with the same slow, powerful resolution. I brought a pot of coffee, and he drained all eight cups, one right after another. Then without pausing to digest, he picked up his shovel. Before digging the first shovelful, he gave me the briefest glance, saying, "Thankee, ma'am."

I had the most ridiculous, euphoric feeling of being thrilled by his recognition.

Wilson had twenty feet of the line dug. I was hacking at some of my favorite weeds at one corner of our house when I noticed my two small sons stalk outside to observe the action.

I watched anxiously from around the corner. I had seen many workers disturbed by onlookers, especially women, and more especially children. Wilson did not stop working or even slow down, but between shovelsful of gooky muck, I could see a conversation taking place which continued for an amazingly long time. Then my sons nonchalantly wandered away. Driven with curiosity, I interrogated them.

"Oh, we like him," said the oldest child noncommittally.

"He's Wee Willy," said the younger.

"That's what we're supposed to call him."

"He's a funny man, all right."

And that was all I could ferret out of those blasted little male minds.

My husband arrived home at dusk. The time was late for a working man, but Wilson was still digging. Gene pitched in and by midnight, after another huge dinner for everyone, we had running water.

The whole affair seemed so ordinary. Just digging out and replacing a rusted water pipe. But Wilson had an uncommon air about him.

I knew Gene liked and respected this waddling hunk of man, and I was just beginning to discover why.

I was more or less pregnant again. After a few short weeks of living on the farm, we settled into a daily routine that started in the early hours with milking and feeding the stock, followed by a hearty breakfast. My husband left for the factory by seven. Much to my surprise, rising before dawn was a pleasure. Seldom was there any wind at five a.m., so the prairie was quiet except for the chuckle and whir of quail rustling through the tall grass down the hill. I loved to stop in the little cow barn while Gene was milking. The warmth of the animals, their breath steaming in the cold air, the rich aroma of a special feed that smelled like molasses, and the squirting of rich milk into a big, sparkling-clean pail were the sights and sounds and smells of a wonderfully satisfying way of life. Gene carried the huge pail brimming with golden milk to our milk shed where the contents became my responsibility. I poured milk into settling pans for the cream to rise. I carefully scraped off the thick cream and made butter, added cream to homemade cottage cheese, filled milk pitchers for cereal, and made whipped-cream cakes just to use up the luscious stuff. What we could not finish ourselves, I gave away or occasionally sold. How delighted I was to finally purchase a secondhand restaurant refrigerator with two doors for twenty-five dollars. I could store gallons of fresh cream, which would remain sweet for three weeks.

The word *cholesterol* had not become popular, thank heavens. We never counted calories, for we were far too busy. Excess poundage simply never appeared. I had learned to hook and throw a bale of hay and to assist Gene in even the most physical chores. With the war on, there were no farmhands available. We were the farmhands, so we blissfully consumed all those yummy calories without any dire consequences.

My big job — with which I got no help from my husband — was to care for the chickens. Chickens must be the least intelligent of all farm animals. I felt no sympathy for them. Each morning after Gene was off to fight his war and the children were fed, I went to the chicken house with my mop and bucket. Swabbing up after those dirty birds was an endless, thankless chore I never could learn to enjoy. As stupid as those chickens were, I'm certain they sensed my feelings toward them. The minute I entered their home, the inhabitants squawked and fluttered all over the place. And that's not all they did all over the place! The roosters strutted around just daring me to touch them. And touch them I did. It never bothered me one tiny bit to snatch up one of these guys, chop off his egotistical head, and dip his inert body in scalding water to start the process of stripping feathers.

One evening, Gene and I began poring over a collection of tractor catalogs. He had prepared charts comparing fuel consumption, horsepower, and prices. I almost expected him to order a recording of each tractor's engine so he could make a comparison of motor noise.

Finally Gene made his decision and filled in all the forms for a Sears model. Since he was happy, I was delighted, for I could envision this big tractor shoving all that slush pit muck down into the dry hole in the front yard.

By this time I was much more pregnant than less, and one afternoon in April I realized the time had arrived for my trip to the hospital. After a relatively easy labor, I gave birth to another magnificent male child. Then I had to suffer through an enforced vacation of ten boring days in the hospital.

Visiting hours brought my husband with questions about our new son, a handsome specimen of eight wiggly pounds. Gene could see him only through thick glass, which was not only unsatisfactory but frustrating. He was eager to hold the baby, hear him breathe, and watch him stretch and gurgle. There is great pleasure in watching a man with his child, and Gene was a most intense parent. He was so elated with this third son that he began talking about a fourth child. I said nothing.

The interminable ten days ended. My son and I were driven home by a close friend. She had prepared our dinner and left after she saw that I was comfortable and settled. I was alone with my three sons but felt at ease and secure. I looked forward to the evening and my husband's arrival.

During the afternoon a delivery truck appeared. The driver announced he had a Sears tractor aboard. Where did I want the crates?

I looked at the man. I looked at the truck. Crates?

"Just unload them on the ground where you're parked," I said.

The tractor was in pieces, crated in five wooden boxes. I walked around them, frowning. They seemed disappointingly small. I asked the man if he was sure everything was here. He just stared at me, quite obviously miffed that this dumb housewife should question his performance as a delivery man. He simply didn't realize that I was expecting to see a big, fine John Deere or Massey-Ferguson monster roar out the back of his truck.

He jammed a piece of paper under my nose, and I signed it. I returned to the house, straightened a few cushions, checked the prepared dinner, and read to the older boys. How pleasant it was to be home! I brushed my hair and put on a trace of lipstick. At 6:30 Gene rumbled down the driveway in the old red pickup. I grabbed our newborn son and walked outside to greet the proud father.

"The tractor!" he yelled, screeching his pickup to a halt beside the crates. "It's arrived! Call Wilson."

I gazed at my husband for a few seconds. He had his knife out and was excitedly slicing through those damn crates. Very quickly he found instruction sheets, sat on one crate and started reading. I knew I had lost him. He was too excited even to give me a peck on the cheek to welcome me home after ten days — nor was he interested in holding his new son. I hugged the baby close, turned around, walked inside, and called Willy Wilson.

Willy waddled down the road immediately. The two men began pulling out all the brightly painted parts and before dark actually had the thing stuck together. To my surprise it looked exactly like a tractor, only in miniature. Warily I watched my husband gazing at it. I had a strange feeling that this little machine was casting a spell over him like some brazen hussy — right in front of me. She was dressed in bright red, had a small seat that held my husband in a loving embrace, and sported two cute little headlights — I could have scratched out those lights in an instant. The green-eyed monster of jealousy was sitting on my shoulder urging me into further mean thoughts. In the dim evening I could have sworn that tractor blinked long black eyelashes at me with a smug smirk.

58

Inside the house, I settled my new son and finished preparing dinner. If my husband didn't come in by eight o'clock, I decided, dinner would be beer and peanut butter sandwiches for him. Eight o'clock came and went.

Promptly at nine o'clock I saw Gene lovingly wrap a rope around something in Little Red Hussy's engine. Then he gave a mighty yank. I was astonished to hear a sudden loud putt, putt, putt. Willy Wilson fiddled with the controls and before long the putt, putt, putt sped up. I could just barely hear my husband yell, "She's running!" over the harsh roar of that objectionable creature.

Little Red Hussy's lights twinkled, and I had to stand at the window and watch my husband ride her around our front yard. What a treat for them both! I hoped he would fall off. Then Gene gallantly offered Wilson a turn, but Wilson declined. Little Red Hussy, I could see, was going to be a one-man tractor.

At long last Gene came inside for his beer and peanut butter sandwiches. After he seemed satisfied, I brought out our youngest son for a feeding.

"This," I said with a tinge of sarcasm, "is our third and *final* son."

"He looks fine," my husband replied. "Do you realize that at 2,500 rpm our tractor generates an even five horsepower?"

"How fascinating!" I almost screamed. *Our* tractor indeed! "Here, you may now burp *your* third and final son."

My husband expertly accepted his tiny son into his arms. I heard a little burp, then watched Gene try his favorite trick with babies. He had moved to a comfortable wicker rocker with big arms. With one elbow propped up on the wicker arm, he tilted the baby just enough to place his ear over the tiny tummy. Then he gave the baby a gentle shake to see if there was still a gurgle. At that point, *my* beautiful third and final son threw up all over my husband's head and into every crevice of that wicker rocker.

I smiled. Justice had been accomplished. I took this promising young man from his father and cuddled him lovingly until he fell into a peaceful sleep.

But I continued to feel uneasy over the time and emotion that Little Red Hussy demanded of my husband. She was soon fitted with a real plow, a disk, and a vast array of fashionable accessories most women can only hope for. Her wardrobe was more complete than mine. I was informed that all these items were needed if we were to convert our farm into a veritable Garden of Eden. All I wanted was some green grass in place of that yawning hole in the front yard.

The war had more and more impact on our lives as the months passed. Government-imposed rationing came, and within a matter of days, if a line formed anywhere, I joined the end, asked what we were waiting for, and patiently jostled and joked my way to the front. America was capable of producing both guns and butter, and everyone accepted rationing as reasonable and necessary. Our shortages were minimal in comparison to those of any other country. During my World War I infancy, sugar was a scarce item, and I was taught to eat my cereal without it. I knew we had to be ready for unexpected scarcities caused by World War II.

Gasoline was the scarce item this time around. Our farm location required extensive driving, and Gene was extremely concerned that I should never feel isolated. Werewolves, remember? With the new restrictions caused by rationing, my attitude towards the Little Red Hussy underwent a profound change. Books with stamps were issued for gasoline rationing, and Gene found he could apply for farm gasoline to run his dear little tractor. He arrived home with a fistful of extra stamps. It wasn't long before I discovered that our service-station attendant didn't mind whether he put that agricultural gasoline directly into my car's tank or the Little Red Hussy's.

I could never quite forgive Little Red Hussy's brash arrival, but she drank very little gas herself because she had only one piston instead of four.

"What ever happened to her other three pistons?" I impishly asked my husband one evening.

"What do you care now that you're drowning in gasoline?"

I had no swift retort for my husband over that stroke of good luck.

FOUR

MOONSHINE
AND MYRTIE

The telephone rang, Gene answered, and after a few pleasant words hung up with a smile. "Honey, Larry and Sondra Travers want to drive out and christen our farm."

My chores were finished, the older boys fed, the baby in bed. We had seen none of our friends for weeks and I was in the mood for some gaiety. I loved the Traverses. They were a delightful, sophisticated couple. Larry had worked every kind of job from bricklayer to messenger boy but was now a successful lawyer with a warm, generous personality that drew people to him. Our sons attached themselves to this man the minute he walked in our door. Larry looked like an uncle. He had a smashed-in nose that made him ruggedly handsome. His voice was deep and positive and must have sounded most convincing in a courtroom.

Our farm had had such chaotic impact on Polly Heddlestone that I was nervous over Sondra's first visit. She was what I considered really "swish." Always dressed in the latest fashion with great taste, she stood out in any group. Her hair was jet black, brushed straight back into a beautiful figure eight at the nape of her neck. Sondra had worked in Chicago and New York City and was a highly competent executive secretary to an oil man in Tulsa. She smoked, drank Scotch on the rocks, read all the latest books, and was a great conversationalist. The Traverses had no children, so we knew it would be just a matter of time before the draft took Larry.

Sondra stepped out of their car dressed in the latest fashion for farming — well-cut, expensive, corduroy slacks and walking shoes. I breathed a sigh of relief. They presented us with a thirteen-dollar bottle of bootleg Teacher's Highland Cream. This was a great gift in dry Oklahoma, and a luxury we had not been able to afford for some time. Drinks were quickly mixed. For once the wind was gentle, so we sat outside in the quiet afternoon to watch a golden Oklahoma sunset spread across the sky. The war seemed very far away.

Larry and Sondra wanted to inspect our farm. With drinks in hand, we wandered towards the chicken house. I was still apprehensive over their reaction to the pervasive aroma of fresh chicken droppings, but I had scrubbed the place early that morning. Their first question was a pleasant surprise.

"So this is a real business with you country folks?" said Larry admiringly. I giggled modestly.

"The market's improving constantly," observed Gene. "People have to eat to win this war. Believe me, the Depression has disappeared." I was beginning to hate that word *Depression*, and I was glad it was finally receding.

"This calls for a baptism," said Larry. He uncorked that beautiful bottle of Scotch and splashed a tiny bit right on top of one of my hens. The chicken squawked and fluttered off to a dark corner of the chicken house.

"Don't waste too much on those blasted chickens!" I gasped.

"Right," laughed Larry. "It's the spirit that counts."

We all agreed and splashed a little more Scotch into our glasses. Larry announced he would soon be off to the military — he had joined the Judge Advocate General's Corps. Larry was one of the few men in the Army placed exactly where he should be. Even though this form of practicing law could be extremely boring, Larry would do well and return alive and whole.

Sondra observed my chickens with fascination. Finally she drew me aside and in a sincere, pleading tone asked, "When do we get to pick the eggs?"

Pick the eggs? I broke into delighted laughter. "We just 'pick' the eggs once a day, in the morning. But they're dirty, you know. I have to wash them all."

"Darn! I wish I could help," said Sondra. I believe she meant it.

Then we checked the pigpen, which was strictly my husband's territory. Sometimes when necessary I threw garbage at the pigs — and I mean *threw* — but I never dared get too close to that pen.

"Watch this," said Gene. He stepped over the low fence. The pigs paid little attention, accepting him as one of their own. He walked up to a particularly friendly looking pig and scratched the beast's ear, then chucked him under the chin. I had never seen this trick before. That pig was actually smiling and rubbing against Gene's leg.

"I can't stand this," laughed Sondra.

"You haven't seen anything yet," Gene smirked, enjoying this chance to show off for city friends. He then scratched this silly, smiling pig under the tummy. The pig flopped down on one side, then over on his back with all four feet in the air. That shoat must have believed he was in hog heaven.

"How terrible!" squealed Sondra in mock horror. "You're scratching your own bacon! How can you ever think of eating that pig?"

"This is a special pig," smiled Gene, quite pleased with the whole drama. "I'll probably sell him."

"You could at least use him for breeding," Sondra protested. "I mean, my God, give him his day in the sun."

"That's impossible. This one's been castrated."

"Been what?!"

"Makes them grow faster."

"I'll never eat pork again," said Sondra.

We sauntered across the pasture where our two cows grazed. "The grass is holding its own," said my husband.

"How can you tell?" asked Sondra.

"Oh, just by looking."

"Hm, looks weedy to me. I thought grass was simply grass," said Sondra.

"That's what most people think," pronounced my husband sagely. By this time he had Sondra believing everything he said. "Say, I could crank up my new tractor, and we all can take turns riding it."

I froze with jealousy.

"Hey, that sounds —" Larry started to say.

"We'll pass on that one," broke in Sondra quickly. I could have hugged her. "We certainly don't want to be arrested for drunken tractor driving. What if we ran over a cow and turned her into hamburger?"

I was beginning to relax. We hadn't scared off all our city friends. In fact, Larry and Sondra were definitely interested in our new life.

"How about a drink at our local bar and grill?" asked my husband.

"Why do you think we drove all the way out here?" laughed Sondra.

"Not that we haven't been drinking," grinned Larry. "Of course, I have to get in training. I hear that JAG officers work six hours a day and can buy a fine bottle of Scotch, legally, for three dollars!"

"A tough way to fight a war," observed my husband.

"Lawyers are useless," said Larry. "We could negotiate the enemy to death, but the Japs and Krauts aren't in a talking mood yet."

"Enough war talk!" protested Sondra. "This is practically Larry's farewell party. Where is this local speakeasy you've been talking about?"

Quickly I called a neighborhood girl from down the hill to stay with the boys. I could hardly wait to be off — preacher's daughter or not. Prohibition may have been lifted from most of the country, but Oklahoma was still officially "bone dry" and was to remain so for years to come. Those of us who enjoyed an occasional drink before packaged liquor was legalized used the services of our friendly local bootlegger. When we had enough money for a case of liquor, we called him on the phone. He came to the back door, carefully put the bottles in the household liquor cabinet, was paid in cash, tipped his hat, and left. Usually our bootlegger was accompanied by his well-mannered young son.

We rarely drank outside our home, but for those who did, Oklahoma offered a wide variety of speakeasies, sometimes in old farmhouses in the country. I had never visited one of those notorious establishments. With two officers of the court — Mr. Larry Travers and my husband — Sondra and I tripped merrily towards our local speakeasy. My curiosity was about to explode.

"Which neighbor has this speakeasy?" I asked.

"You'll see," replied Gene, intent on playing his little game. We decided to walk. Gene, the intrepid pathfinder, stopped at two little ruts disappearing into a grove of trees. I had always been curious about that little grove — but also a bit frightened.

We started walking along the two ruts.

"This is spooky," whispered Sondra. Larry grabbed her to emphasize how well he could take care of the situation, then laughed. "Looks okay to me," he drawled in his typically make-out-all-right manner. If I were a soldier, I thought to myself with an appreciative glance at Larry, he would be my first choice for a buddy. I knew he would always remain cool, whatever the circumstances.

The sun had set, and we were surrounded by soft dusk. There was sufficient light to see a little wooden house — really a shack — through the trees at the end of the ruts. As we walked closer, I could see a couple of geese, a few chickens pecking around, three pigs, four dogs, a flock of guinea hens, two goats, one huge turkey, and one peacock — then I lost count. Every animal was on the loose. I could see no fence. By the appearance of the house I would guess the owners, whoever they were, could not afford a fence. But that didn't seem to matter to the animals.

The door of the house opened, and there stood Willy Wilson, all 220, short, stocky pounds of him.

"Hidy folks!" he yelled, with a grin I had never seen on him before. This was a different Willy and a funny one, too. I knew vaguely he lived in this area, but my life had been far too busy to find the exact location.

Now I began to understand. The Depression was over — for most people. But not for Willy Wilson and his family. They owned only five acres and had struggled to pay taxes even on that small plot.

There was no way Wilson could hold a regular job because his plumbing skills were adapted to this neck of the woods, not to city codes. Willy picked up what odd jobs he could from neighbors like my husband who were too busy to tend their farms. I could see a stack of rabbit hutches, and I conjectured that rabbits brought in a little spending money. And now the Wilson home was Wilson's Bar and Grill.

Willy welcomed us into his living room which was set up for business. There were three old but comfortable-looking sofas, two low coffee tables, lamps with dim bulbs, and a large clean rag rug on the floor. I wanted to call it a parlor. The hand-me-down furniture reminded me of parsonage life.

We all felt instantly relaxed and at home. I heard the floor in the kitchen squeak, and a new face appeared at the door.

"Meet Myrtie!" exclaimed Wilson. Myrtie was exactly the height of Willy, but she weighed a little more — right at 250 pounds was my guess.

"You must be our new neighbors!" she hollered. Myrtie moved towards me like a tank and enveloped me in a crushing hug. "You've come to the right place, honey. We make the best goddamned moonshine in the county!"

Oh my. What a neighbor! I checked my ribs carefully but they all seemed to be intact.

"What'll it be, folks?" asked Myrtie. "Moonshine and soda or moonshine and Coke? Or maybe somebody thinks he's a real tough son-of-a-bitch and wants a straight shot!" She laughed heartily, and all 250 pounds quivered.

I couldn't take my eyes off Myrtie. Gene advised me to begin with a little moonshine and Coke until I understood what this stuff could do. Sondra and my husband opted for moonshine and soda. Larry said he liked his moonshine on the rocks.

Myrtie gave Larry a little wink, repeating, "On the rocks — huh!" I could tell she appreciated his mettle. She disappeared into the kitchen. Thirty seconds later, I heard her booming voice, "Wee Willy, get your ass in here!"

Wee Willy took his own sweet time, but he did go. I listened intently but couldn't hear a word. Finally Willy reappeared saying, "Folks, we're out of booze. Gotta check out the vault."

66

"Can we come along?" pleaded Sondra.

"Sure," said Willy. "You can be my lookout. If you see a cloud of dust coming down the road, holler."

Sondra was ecstatic. We all trooped back of the house into a large garden where the Wilsons grew potatoes, corn, green beans, carrots, and lettuce.

"Any sign of the law?" whispered Willy.

"No — no!" said Sondra glancing around. Suddenly it was no joking matter. Wilson dug into the fresh dirt. I heard the soft clink of his shovel against glass. He reached down and pulled out a quart fruit jar full of clear liquid. The jar was sealed tight with a canning lid.

Larry laughed right out loud. "I've heard of garden vaults for moonshine. At last I've seen the real thing. Now I can die a happy man."

"A garden is always being dug in, right?" said Willy. "No copper I've ever known is going to get his mitts dirty, and I won't loan out my shovel without a warrant."

We all returned to the parlor, thirsty and eager for a drink after our secretive excursion.

Larry Travers sipped gingerly at his moonshine on the rocks. "Damned good stuff," he said, mildly surprised.

"Bet your ass," chimed in Myrtie. "I don't believe in serving horse piss to paying guests."

Sondra practically choked, but she was loving every minute. With flesh-and-blood people like the Wilsons, who needed movies?

I knew Myrtie and Willy had four grown sons — all of military age. With my three sons only knee-high, I felt more than a pang of concern for the Wilsons. Finally I had to ask, "Have you heard from your boys?"

"Goddamned right," said Myrtie. "We got it all down in code. See, you can't say nothin' in a letter about where you're at, or else the crap'll hit the fan. So we got the whole Pacific and all of Europe and most of Africa drawed up like a great big farm. Sheep is for England and the Philippines is chickens and Hawaii is peacocks and Australia is pigs. If the sheep are putting on a heavy coat, it's the north of England. We talk about all different animals and how many we got, like meaning how long have you been there, and so on. Then all I have to do is read the newspaper to know what action is going on, and then I can know exactly what my boys are into."

"I didn't know they would take all the boys of one family," said Larry.

"Shucks, them sons-of-bitches all ran out and volunteered," said Myrtie. "They're havin' the time of their lives, sailing into foreign ports, drinking up a storm, chasing all the skirts. I know them rascals. But I sure do feel sorry for them German and Jap mothers and fathers 'cause we're gonna kick the ever-loving shit out of those dumb bastards!"

This time I was really shocked by Myrtie's outburst. And until that moment I had never quite thought of Japanese and German parents in such a personal way. My face must have reflected my feelings. Myrtie came over to me and enveloped me in another 250-pound hug. "Now, honey, don't take no offense at the way I talk — I know it's different. Just cain't get the grammar right. My daddy was a sailor man, and I was right proud of the son-of-a-bitch even if he couldn't talk too good. I grew up in Panama guarding the god-damned canal. Let me tell you one thing — before I hitched up with Wee Willy here, I had me one hell of a time as a little sister screwing around them docks and locks with all those crazy sailor boys."

As I reeled from this portrait of a life I'd never known, Myrtie lay back her head and laughed. She shook, the sofa shook, the floor shook, the whole house shook.

"But my Willy here is the real hero," said Myrtie, suddenly becoming serious. "Aren't you? Tell our payin' guests what you done in the Great War."

"I ain't gonna tell nothin'," protested Wee Willy.

"Then I am. Willy here stumbled into a German machine-gun nest back in '18. Had nothing with him but a shovel like the dumb farmer he was then. It was a mistake, of course, but it was too late to back out easy. Since he didn't have a whole lot of choice, he started whomping the crap out of seven Huns, one right after the another, real methodi-cal like. He got the Silver Star for it. Go git your star, Willy."

"I will not," said Wilson firmly.

"He shoulda got the Medal of Honor, but he came out of that German nest without a scratch on his body. You gotta git shot all to hell before you git a Medal of Honor."

"That ain't true, Myrtie."

"The hell it ain't."

"With this code of yours," said Larry, searching for a way out of this uneasy argument, "you must know more about this war than we can read in the newspapers."

"That's the goddamned truth," said Myrtie. "And we're sure teaching them censoring officers a whole lot about farming."

"Well, I'm going into the JAG in two weeks," said Larry. "I'm afraid it won't be very exciting, though."

"I hope not," said Sondra.

"I've got nothing against lawyers and JAG officers," said Myrtie. "Just don't go throwing my boys into the stockade for a little bar fighting now and then."

Larry looked up at Myrtie keenly. "Don't worry. I'll get myself on the defense side."

The phone rang. Myrtie answered it, listened, and then said, "Thanks a million, honey."

I saw Willy's eyes fix on Myrtie. "Was that Sarah?" he asked.

"Yep," said Myrtie. Then turning to us, she said, "Folks, let me get you another drink. We're gonna have a raid."

"Another *drink?*" I gasped. "We'll all be arrested — "

"Don't fret none, honey," said Myrtie. "Just sit back and relax."

"Did you arrange this especially for us?" asked Sondra.

"I sure as hell didn't," explained Myrtie. "That was Sarah down at the courthouse. She works as a cleaning woman a couple nights a week like I used to before the war. She keeps me up on what's going on."

"How about another quick round of drinks and some of Myrtie's chili?" asked my husband.

"Mexican or gringo style?" asked Myrtie.

"We'd better go gringo," cautioned my husband. "Myrtie's Mexican chili is the real thing."

It wasn't long before we heard a heavy knock on the door. We sat frozen while Willy ushered in two uniformed county deputy sheriffs.

"Don't mind us, folks," said one.

The other looked around, saying, "This is a raid. Don't seem to see any bootleg hooch anywhere."

Neither of them was looking for anything. Willy Wilson was just standing there very patiently. I could hear Myrtie bustling around in the kitchen. She brought out our chili, then walked up to the two deputies. She pulled two half-pint bottles out of a large pocket in her dingy dress. "Here, boys. Now git your asses off my property. Cain't you see we got company?"

"Sure, ma'am."

"Sorry, ma'am. Until next time."

We watched them go.

"That's what you get for making the best goddamned moonshine in the county," said Myrtie.

Larry Travers was shaking his head. "And you just put up with this?"

"You got another way, lemme know real quick," remarked Myrtie.

"I don't know of another way," said Larry. "But it doesn't seem quite right."

"I suppose this is a matter of rendering unto Caesar what is Caesar's," I said.

"Honey," said Myrtie, "I don't know a goddamned thing about Mr. Caesar."

Our living room with its beamed ceiling and knotty-pine walls quickly took on a warm, personal character. Visitors felt comfortably absorbed into its coziness. We — that is, I — trucked in cord after cord of hickory and oak firewood to feed the fireplace. From early fall to late spring we always had a fire going. In fact, that fireplace was the only heat for the entire house.

That had not been our intention. We installed a floor furnace in the bedroom/kitchen area with the idea that we could pipe in the natural gas from our oil well. No gas bill to pay! It didn't work out that way. Other wells in the Airport Pool produced gas that a few of our neighbors used to heat and even light their houses. Our oil well snubbed us — no gas. I was beginning to regret this whole dumb oil business. I cooked with butane, but it was much too expensive to use

70

in a floor furnace. The only alternative was our huge fireplace. When bedtime arrived, I donned my nightgown in front of the hearth, then ran into the cold bedroom, jumped into bed, and rubbed the sheets with my feet to get warm. Most parsonages had cold bedrooms, so I was used to this. Only now I had a husband to snuggle with under all those covers.

A big wood fire radiates a cozy warmth no other heating source can produce. What fun our sons had toasting marshmallows and occasionally baking eggs in the ashes. Our first winter was unusually windy and cold. We consumed thirty-two cords of firewood at two-and-a-half dollars per cord. To get wood at that price, I drove the red pickup fifteen miles north of Tulsa to a wooded farm outside Turley. Gasoline was still cheap and so was my labor, for I loaded all thirty-two cords myself. I wore heavy leather gloves, two sweaters, my thick wool Pendleton pants, and cowboy boots — plus a tam pulled down tightly over my ears. Even my mother would not have recognized me and I would have avoided her anyway, for this was no ladylike job. My only concern was that tossing all that firewood into the back of my pickup might turn me into another Myrtie Wilson. Much as I adored her, I had no desire to develop her muscles and huge stomach.

If our living room with its fireplace was heaven, then the kitchen was hell. With all due respect to Deke and my husband, that room was small, dark, and uninviting. The walls had no insulation to keep out the winter cold, the floor was like a sheet of ice, and the windows and doors were like sieves. A blue norther would swirl out of Canada, gather force through North and South Dakota, Nebraska, and Kansas, then blow straight through my kitchen.

Each winter morning I put on layers of shirts, pants, socks, and a robe, waddled into our freezing kitchen, and fired up the stove. I will say that my range was a tip-top model — a Detroit Jewel with a high oven, thermostat, broiler, and four burners. I turned on each burner full strength and opened the door of the oven. I pulled my tam down tighter and started the big breakfast I knew Gene needed after milking the cows and slopping those grinning pigs. As I shivered and cooked, I pictured him down there in his cozy barn with the heat radiating from all those warm bodies in their furry winter coats.

Little did I know that I too had furry company, until one day I saw evidence of mice. I wasted no time setting out traps. The latest thing was to use peanut butter. Mice are nutty about the stuff and can detect the aroma clear across an open field. The peanut butter worked. One morning I caught two tiny baby mice in one trap. Gene had never heard of catching two at one time. He was gleeful over my great success, but I was stricken with guilt. All I could think of were those two little trusting baby mice — probably brother and sister — cozying up for a joint nibble. Then whack! The deadly trap slaughtered them both.

My softhearted attitude toward rodents was soon to change. We eliminated the mice, and everything was just dandy for several weeks. Then one bitterly cold morning when Canada had just sent down one of its first-class blue northers, I struggled clumsily into the kitchen in my many layers of clothes. I lighted the stove as usual, turned around, and opened a lower cabinet door. There stood a huge rat! This beast stared up at me defiantly. I screamed at the top of my Methodist hymn-singing voice. Fortunately Gene had not yet gone to his milking. He ran into the kitchen like a shot, grabbed a long cooking fork, and lunged at the rat. He jabbed, and one of the prongs pierced right through the rat's neck. The skewered beast flailed at the fork, curving his hideous rat body around one side like a snake. I was mesmerized.

"Fill a pan with water!" Gene shouted.

I started with a jerk, grabbed a big pan, and with trembling hands turned on the faucet. Thank God the pipes hadn't frozen! I watched Gene maneuver the struggling rat to the edge of the shelf.

"Hold the pan steady — right next to the shelf," he said quietly.

I shivered and so did the pan, causing water to slosh over my feet. Suddenly Gene skidded the rat off the shelf. With a great splash he plunged the thrashing animal deep into the water. I almost dropped the pan. I was numb with terror. Gene grabbed the pan with one hand and eased it steadily to the floor while I watched the water swirl and foam.

The rat was dead. I walked through the motions of preparing breakfast as if I were in a trance. My husband gave me a reassurring little good-bye kiss and left for work. Still distracted, I put my sons into the truck and drove to Turley to load another cord of firewood. Each time I tossed a log into the back of the truck, I imagined I was throwing it at the rat. The old man who sold the firewood was so impressed he offered me a job. "All the young fellows — they're gone," he drawled. "You load right smart."

I thanked him but declined his offer. My husband was bringing in the money; I was merely supplying the manual labor. As I drove home I wondered why in all my husband's lectures about the joys of agrarian life, I'd never heard any mention of rats.

The next morning I insisted that Gene check out the kitchen first, saying, "I'm a coward when it comes to rats, and I don't mind admitting it." He cheerfully agreed, laughing, sure there would not be another —

"RAT!" he yelled. A gigantic rat was standing stock-still next to the stove. It must have been looking for its mate. I looked anxiously at Gene as I climbed on a chair, then yelled at the boys to stay out. That rat looked right at me with nasty little beady eyes. I felt as though we were being stalked by a prehistoric animal. Suddenly Gene leaped forward, kicking at the rat. The rat counterattacked, biting at my husband's ankle.

"Watch out!" I screamed, but it was too late. Gene swung his right foot, and I could see that the rat's dirty yellow teeth had only caught his sock. Thank God for that! The rat suddenly let go and fell on its side right in the middle of my kitchen. Gene now became a raging fury. He jumped on the rat before it could regain its senses. He stamped on it like a man gone wild — stamped on it until the whole kitchen shook. Finally, when he was convinced he'd killed it, he sat down at the kitchen table, trembling. Quickly I jumped off the chair, poured him a glass of water, and started coffee.

"We've got to do something about these rats," I said. "If one of our children wandered in here, a rat could kill him. Besides, we could all be wiped out with bubonic plague."

My shaken husband agreed in a barely audible voice. He sat there until his trembling stopped and the color returned to his face.

"I must hurry to the factory," he said at last. "Call Wilson and tell him we need a rat-killing scat-cat."

"A scat-cat?" I asked, puzzled.

73

"Wilson will explain," he said on his way out the door. "You handle it."

I called Willy Wilson and told him about our rat problem.

"Just keep a .22 automatic rifle handy," he advised. "Them hollow points blows up a rat real good."

"A gun?" I said, startled. "What if I miss? I'll shoot up the kitchen floor."

"Only makes a little bitty hole," said Wilson. "Besides, Myrtie don't miss very often."

I believed him. Although I could shoot a little, I wasn't about to start putting holes in my kitchen floor, no matter how little bitty. "My husband wants a scat-cat . . . whatever that is."

"Oh, one of those, eh?" said Wilson. "'Kay. I'll gitcha a real mean one."

Wilson showed up later that morning with an old lady's hatbox under his arm. I could hear something inside snarling and hissing like a bobcat.

"This here's a goodern," announced Wilson. "I'm gonna let him go now." He opened the box and a wild streak of gray flashed straight up in the air.

"Scat! Cat!" yelled Wilson, hitting at the gray lightning.

It was the biggest and toughest old tomcat I'd ever seen. I caught a glimpse of its yellow eyes as it dashed off down the hill to the cowshed.

"Now there are strict rules about owning a scat-cat," explained Wilson. "You treat him bad as you can. Don't give him a single scrap of food. Every time he comes up near the house, scat him away. What you're doing is forcing him to make his living off of rats. Pretty soon a good rat-killer like this one will start killing rats for sport."

I desperately wanted to protest this outrageous treatment. "Does he have a name?" was all I could ask.

"Now don't go coddling him. It's your kids against them dirty, filthy rats. Old Tom is on your side. Call him Scat-cat or Old Tom, but don't go giving him a real name."

Willy Wilson was very convincing. I agreed to keep my broom handy. But whaling a cat with a broom seemed like an odd way to protect my children from rats.

"Oh, and tell your husband the game is on for tonight," said Wilson picking up the empty hatbox.

"What game?" I asked, innocently enough.

"Ask him," said Wilson with the tiniest hint of a smile on his rough face. "I'm sure he can explain something."

Explain something! It was against my nature to become a suspicious wife. But that "something" in Wilson's hint of a smile made me uneasy and, well, suspicious.

When Gene arrived home at his usual late hour, I reported about Old Tom. I proudly explained that I'd already whacked him twice with my broom. Then I casually relayed Wilson's message about the "game."

"What game is this?" I asked as nonchalantly as possible.

"Just a little poker game."

My first reaction was not to worry. Once or twice a month my husband had a group of men out to our place for a friendly game while I would go to town and play bridge. We saved on baby-sitters with this method. There was no drinking during these poker games, and stakes were small. When I returned home I always made hot cocoa and served the men cookies. That was my view of poker.

My husband was a good player. He almost always managed to leave the table with a few dollars more than he had when the evening began. As a gin rummy and bridge player, I had some idea about poker, for Gene had taught me the basic rules. But I was no expert concerning questions of bluffing, the famous poker face, and all those other masculine subtleties.

Somehow, the more I mulled over this prospective poker game at Wilson's, the more uneasy I became. The Wilsons served liquor as a business. Finally I inquired ever so gently into the scope of this "game."

"Nothing much," said my husband. "Wilson doesn't play himself. He just sets up the game and takes twenty cents out of each pot for the house."

Well, that seemed straightforward enough. "And who exactly does he invite to these poker games?" I asked.

"Different men," answered my husband.

"Strangers?"

"Sometimes."

I vowed I would not interfere. But not interfering did not mean I was unconcerned. Gene disappeared immediately after dinner and did not reappear until just after midnight. He chose not to give me a detailed report. In fact, you might say he was using his skills at home — his poker face was completely impassive. My curiosity, which had always been prodigious, would just have to simmer.

A month dragged by with Gene disappearing down the road toward the Wilsons' two evenings a week. My curiosity was not the only thing simmering. I began to entertain vague fears of our house and property coming into play. I'd read English novels in which impetuous young lords threw the deeds to their estates into the pot to cover their bets.

One Sunday I awakened at two o'clock in the morning. No husband. I sat straight up. This time I was really frightened. I wondered if the whole farm would disappear at that poker table. Besides, how can a man hold down a full-time job and stay up so late? Finally I heard Gene slip into the house and quietly get ready for bed. Not a word was said.

I had to act. Even though this was a Sunday, Gene was off to the factory. I waited until early afternoon when the boys were settled down for a nap. I packed a quart fruit jar full of rich, fresh cream and walked down our road to the Wilsons'. I had no intention of accusing anybody of anything; I just wanted to sound out Myrtie about what was going on. I knew she would ultimately blab the truth.

When I arrived at their little house, the front door was ajar, and the screen half torn off. A wave of fear washed over me. What had my husband gotten himself into?

Carefully I stepped across the porch, trying not to make any squeaks. I listened, my heart racing, but heard nothing. I edged forward and stepped to the door. A sudden squeak froze me. I was literally panting for breath, but I had to investigate.

I eased my head into the doorway. Nothing. Then I saw Myrtie. All 250 pounds of her was spread over a big, comfortable chair. She had a cup of black coffee in one hand. A spoon rattled in the cup as she took a swallow.

I could see her better now in the dim light. Her mouth was bleeding. She was only half dressed. Her stomach sagged. I was overwhelmed with pity.

"Myrtie, you poor . . . !"

"Hi, honey!" she bellowed. "Is that cream? Bless you, child. Coffee without cream is pure crap to me."

I ran to her, unbelieving, and handed her the jar of cream. She untwisted the cap with a fat hand and spooned out two huge dollops. She stirred and stirred and downed the rest of the coffee in three gulps.

"Honey, would you get me another cup?"

I rushed to do her bidding. She dabbed at her bleeding lip, but made no move to straighten out what was left of her jumbled clothes.

"What happened?" I asked at last.

Myrtie roared with laughter. I was utterly confused.

"Don't know for sure. But I betcha I'm knocked up again. After four boys, I'll probably just go ahead and have another pony prick the fifth time around. God — "

"Myrtie, seriously, are you hurt?"

"Nothing a month or two of bedrest won't cure. I never been to a doctor. My ole Willy is pretty good as a midwife."

"Was it — "

"Willy and me was comin' back from church. We don't go too often, but they had this new preacher. He was ranting and raving about drinking and gambling and pretty soon I was fed up. I grabbed Willy by the arm, and we walked right out of the goddamn church.

"Soon's we got home, I said I wasn't never going to listen to that asinine son-of-a-bitch again. Well, I had a big Sunday dinner all laid out, and me and Willy was about to have at it. Then the damnedest thing — Willy says I shouldn't go around calling men of the cloth asinine sons-of-bitches no matter what they says. I said, 'Willy, you're plumb full of crap!' He reared back and whapped me across the face like I was a goddamned Jap whore. I picked up the slaw bowl and crowned him but good.

"But my old Wee Willy, he's too tough. He had the potato pan and slung it at me and just about busted my shoulder off.

"Just gettin' started, we was. Smashed ever goddamned dish on the table. We was right at midbattle when we crashed into the bedroom. It was twenty years ago that Willy built a special bed strong enough for the two of us. We'd already broke two store-bought beds and were running out of cash.

"Well, honey, the long and short of it is that for the first time in twenty years we broke our own homemade bed. I mean it was the goddamnedest fun around here since the boys partied it up before leaving for the war."

"Where's . . . Willy?" I ventured.

"Out scrounging up lumber to build us a new bed, honey. Come nighttime, a man and woman has got to lay down and go to sleep."

I wandered off in a daze. Myrtie was a whole new world to me. Her use of profanity was fascinating, for the words flowed easily and descriptively. As a child I was not even allowed to say "golly" or "gosh." My father was adamant about such language for two reasons. It was against the Ten Commandments, and besides, he maintained, use of profanity showed a lack of vocabulary. When I was eleven, my mother took me to a local high school play, Booth Tarkington's *Seventeen*. I was captivated by the lead actor, an attractive young man who constantly used the expression "Ye gods!" The following day I scurried alone behind the church, sat down, looked all around and very quietly said, "Ye gods." Nothing happened. I repeated the phrase a bit louder, "Ye gods!" I looked up at the sky — no thunder, no voice of protest. I stood up and very loudly said, "YE GODS!!" I brushed my skirt off and stalked away, a wiser and more experienced little girl.

But I walked home from the Wilsons' without having found out anything about those poker games. That very night Gene left for the Wilsons' and did not return until four o'clock in the morning. I was awake, reading. After all my experiences of the day before, I hadn't been able to sleep a wink. Gene walked in stone sober and very, very tired. He had one hour to rest before milking the cows and then rushing off to the factory to put in a twelve-hour day.

"That's it," he sighed. He pulled out a huge wad of bills and laid it on the bed beside me. I picked it up. The wad was composed of a beautiful array of fives, tens, and twenties. Practically no singles. I was breathless.

"Six hundred dollars," he said. "Now we can bring in a gas pipeline for the whole neighborhood. This money will buy the pipe. Wilson and several other neighbors are going to dig the ditch. Next winter you'll have a warm kitchen."

I was happy, but after such a momentous day, I was also confused and a little frightened. "You didn't lure some city slickers out here to cheat them out of their money, did you?"

"Wilson runs an honest game," grinned my husband. "But there was some heavy drinking and a couple of the players were compulsive types that made for easy pickings. When I won the final pot, I realized how much it would have hurt to lose — and to lose the gas pipeline. Don't worry, Mary, I'm not playing at Willy's anymore."

I sank into my pillow, weak with relief. I knew I was the big winner this night. I had gained both a warm kitchen and an enlightened husband. And as far as I know that poker-financed pipeline is still in operation.

It was 1943. By this time we had settled into some semblance of stability. We had two cows, our chicken operation was thriving, the pig business was profitable, and the rats were under control.

The war had become a permanent part of our lives. With my husband outproducing the Germans and Japanese, and with Myrtie Wilson's tough sons on the front lines, I knew it was just a matter of time until we won.

Although my husband seemed busy producing parts for airplanes, I never actually saw any results. It may sound disloyal, but the Douglas plant had a more dramatic impact on me. From atop our hill, we watched the construction of a 5,000-foot-long building without a single window. There, heavy bombers were made and repaired. I remember the first time I saw a four-engine B-29. It flew right over our farm — only a few hundred yards above us. The noise was deafening. Before long we began to see one B-29 after another — lots and lots of them going out and coming back in for repair.

My older boys were starting school now, and although such playground games as "Bombs over Tokyo" were all the rage, I was satisfied that my children were having a relatively normal childhood. They were in their element looking up carefully at each B-29. They memorized the markings and placement of all the guns and were quick to notice any changes. The wings and bottom of the fuselage were always inspected for bullet holes — and sometimes there were plenty. Then one Saturday afternoon, my children came running inside with the fantastic news that they'd just seen the first B-29 that was painted black on the bottom. "For low-level night raids, of course!" announced my militarily knowledgeable children.

We were enjoying our comfortable, secure way of life, and we certainly weren't looking for complications. Getting into the sheep business just happened.

Among our oldest Tulsa friends were Nat Janco and his wife Agnes. Now, Nat had two unusual characteristics. First, he would seriously consider just about any way of accomplishing something — and he favored a highly individualistic, unorthodox approach. With him, it wasn't a matter of being different. He was simply, naturally, and spontaneously unique. Secondly, he didn't just talk about doing unusual things — he did them.

And so he bought Maizie, a lady sheep, and escorted her to his house right in the middle of a lovely residential section of Tulsa. Nat, you see, had a problem. His backyard was quite large, and he was far too busy to spend time meticulously mowing and trimming all that grass. There were no yardmen available; they'd all been drafted. So he conceived the idea of buying Maizie. She came from the Tulsa stockyards equipped with powerful munching teeth. Nat claimed she was the epitome of ovine femininity. Most important of all, she faithfully chopped her way back and forth across the yard as evenly and neatly as any lawn mower.

All progressed as Nat had planned for one week, until Maizie decided to explore the world. The following day a local columnist reported that a woman had called the newspaper to complain about a sheep grazing in her front yard. The columnist wrote further that the astonished woman had called the dog pound. Men arrived in a truck, roped poor Maizie, and carted her off to a canine prison with a bunch of mangy dogs as cell mates. Nat was frantic. He made several phone calls to confirm the story, then raced to the dog pound, posted bond, and sprang Maizie.

That evening, while Maizie languished on a chain in Nat's backyard, we had dinner together. Nat could talk of nothing else but his Maizie. Farmer Gene knowingly informed him that the only way to keep Maizie happily domiciled as a mowing machine was to purchase a ram.

The next morning, Nat drove back to the stockyards. He carefully studied all the rams in the holding pens and finally chose Elmer. Elmer was covered with luscious fleece and had a darling little black twinkling nose. He had a most distinguished pedigree and cost fifty dollars. I had to admit Elmer looked every inch the aristocrat. Nat felt certain Maizie couldn't help but fall in love. The pedigree papers were kept on the dining-room table for everyone to inspect.

Elmer and Maizie were instantly compatible and grazed happily side by side. Nat was positive that for the remainder of the war his grass problem was under control.

A slight difficulty developed. Being a typical male, Elmer tended to be a bit more aggressive than Maizie. He adored roses. Elmer recognized no property lines and blithely ate with equal satisfaction from neighbors' plants on both sides.

At three one morning, Nat and Agnes returned from a party. Elmer heard his master and began bleating in a very loud and demanding "baa!" Nat sighed but settled himself in a lawn chair to quiet Elmer. When Nat tried to sneak off to bed, Elmer couldn't be fooled. His protesting baas were obviously going to disturb already upset neighbors. It was not legal to keep farm animals in the city, and Nat had been lucky to get by so far without an official written complaint.

Nat spent the entire night in the lawn chair. When he awakened, stiff and with the morning sun blistering his face, he was ready to admit defeat. His grand plan had failed, and Nat was the first to admit it.

We received a panicked and pleading telephone call. Would we consider giving Elmer and Maizie a home?

Well, we thought, why not give the sheep business a whirl? Maybe Nat's bad luck was our good fortune. I dug out government bulletins on sheep raising and piled them on a table to read. In our exuberance to learn all we could about farming, we'd ordered bulletins on every domesticated animal known to mankind. Quick reading, we figured, would make us old hands at the sheep business. Besides, we were helping a friend in desperate need.

We rattled into town and let down the tailgate in the Jancos' backyard. The four of us pushed and pleaded until Elmer and Maizie hesitantly went up the ramp. Then we trucked Elmer and Maizie to our farm where they seemed quite contented.

Elmer was a fine, vigorous male of his species. We decided he needed more wives. Off we drove to the stockyards where we carefully selected six females. Now Elmer would have a harem. He should be the happiest ram in Tulsa County.

There was an abundance of excellent, fragrant prairie hay for grazing. Gene constructed a small open shed at the bottom of the hill so the sheep had shelter of their own in bad weather.

I reread all the government bulletins very carefully. Somehow I suspected that I would hear that phrase "You take care of it." I wanted to be prepared. One special trick advised by the government was to smear the ram's belly with sticky red paint. This paint in turn rubbed off on the ewe's back and thus one could tell which female had been bred. Very clever! I purchased the red paint. I just hoped Maizie wouldn't sulk and become jealous.

With the operation successfully under way, it seemed we only had to wait a few weeks until there would be flocks of darling little lambs gamboling around us. What a treat for the boys to have a baby lamb to hold and cuddle! I had read that most births occurred in pairs so I began to count — we could have as many as fourteen baby lambs! Our farm was about to become a storybook showcase — just like the Verdigris farm northeast of town.

But the government had not told us the whole truth. To my dismay, I discovered sheep are extremely dumb — dumber, if possible, than chickens. And hideously dirty.

The first blow to my dreams came when Maizie stuck her head through two slats in the fence around the pigs. An irate pig promptly broke her neck.

Poor, cute Maizie! She was bleating helplessly, her lovely head twisted grotesquely to one side. I waited in agony until Gene arrived home. He shot Maizie to put her out of her misery. I wept real tears.

As the days passed, these sheep began looking dirtier and dirtier. One of the most disgusting sights was their behavior each time I drove into our driveway. At the sound of the car, all those sheep suddenly became very excited. They started running around, bumping into each other stupidly, while they blew phlegm out their noses. They bleated loudly — "baa, baa" — then defecated pea-sized pellets all over the place. After putting on this ridiculous show, they all huddled together — just like a bunch of sheep.

Late one night I awakened to hear a distant, mysterious howl. Wolves still roamed rural Oklahoma. A vision of banker Zanis's werewolf flashed through my mind. Gene was out of bed and into his clothes in a flash. "There's your werewolf," he said, reading my thoughts.

He grabbed a rifle and a powerful flashlight and disappeared into the night. "Be careful," I urged, trying to recall if we had a government bulletin on wolves.

I listened intently and at last heard a shot. My husband soon returned. "Did you get the wolf?"

"No," he answered. "But I had to shoot another sheep. The wolf chewed a leg off one of the ewes."

And so we learned, and not in a very pretty way. Once a dog or wolf develops a taste for sheep, he will range for miles trying to satisfy his appetite. The Wilsons usually kept at least two sheep, but they were always close to the house where their own strictly trained dogs provided protection.

In just a few days, we noticed Elmer was not feeling well. In fact, all the sheep looked droopy and discouraged. They were beginning to spend most of the time huddled in their barn. I feared the worst — an epidemic that would kill them all.

The weather became a deciding factor when a norther blew in and knocked over their shed.

After surveying the damage, Gene announced we would have to abandon the sheep business. But the war was going full force and he had to leave for the factory. "You will take care of it, won't you?" Boy, had I heard that one before!

Gene took my car and left me with the rickety old pickup. But he was kind enough to assist me in loading the sheep before he left. Recently he had built a loading chute that could handle anything from pigs to horses. The remaining female sheep, five of them, walked up the chute on their own. Elmer was a shadow of his former self. He couldn't even stand on his own feet. Gene and I struggled together and literally picked up his dirty, defeated body and threw him into the back of the pickup.

My husband glanced nervously at his watch, gave me a peck, and roared off to the war.

I was now alone with an old rattletrap of a truck, a bunch of sick sheep, and three small children.

It was fifteen miles to the Tulsa stockyards. From our farm I had to drive right through the middle of downtown. Regardless of my feelings, my sons were delighted with this adventure. I stuck them into the cab with cookies and listened to their innocent, cheerful babble.

I started driving. Another blasted problem was that the gas gauge had ceased working — a fact Gene had neglected to tell me. I barely coasted into a service station, purchased five gallons of gas, and resolutely headed towards my goal. Suddenly I realized I was on the same street as the Second National Bank. I glanced around, too late to take a side street. What if I had a flat tire or an accident right in front of the bank? Zanis would poke his head out of the lobby, take one snickering look at me with my load of sick sheep and say, "I told you so, I told you so!"

Several miles on the other side of town, the stockyard buildings came into view. I had been to the stockyards with Gene before and had always felt comfortable. The atmosphere was rural, efficient, businesslike, and welcoming. Only one little gnawing fear remained. What if they wouldn't take my sheep? The sheep were completely silent. Even when the truck hit a bump, I couldn't hear a single protesting "baa!" Surely the stockyards wouldn't take dead animals. Then what would I do?

I drove to the unloading dock and asked for Mr. Dobson, the broker Gene had instructed me to find. He appeared and seemed to know my name, but he didn't say much. Dobson instructed me to back my truck against a particular dock. Then he signaled two men to help unload my sheep.

I stood by, in hushed silence. One of the unloaders carried an electric prod. Elmer's wives struggled up the ramp on their own. But Elmer was prostrate, his sad eyes blinking slowly. With a squeamish jump, I watched the man with the electric prod give Elmer a jolt. His eyes widened, and he rose to his feet with an evangelical surge of energy. The unloader guided Elmer skillfully, giving him a jolt each time he faltered. The men standing around treated this activity as very ordinary, but I was rigid with mortification.

At last our dismal sheep were in a holding pen. Elmer flopped down on the concrete floor, exhausted. I approached Dobson. He was very calm and professional. "Just waiting for the postings to arrive from Saint Louis," he said. "About another half hour."

I began to breathe freely and slowly unwound. The boys clustered around, so I took them on a tour. This was their first visit to the stockyards. I'm sure from their viewpoint we were in a zoo, for animals were all in pens and each seemingly glowed with good health. Other farm women were there, too. They were doing the chores while their men were off fighting the war. At least in America we had the sturdy middle-aged men like Dobson and the unloaders to help. The German farm women, we were to learn later, weren't so lucky.

The posting arrived. The auction did not take long. Very soon, Dobson appeared with a slip of paper.

"Take this to the cashier, ma'am. T'aint much, I'm afraid."

I exhaled an immense sigh of relief. Somebody had actually bought our sheep! "My husband called and explained, didn't he?"

"He certainly did, ma'am. He's having real good luck in pigs. Sheep raising is a special business."

I started corralling my sons.

"Fine boys you've got there, ma'am," said Mr. Dobson.

"Why, thanks," I said, looking down at the three little grins. "They've had a wonderful day."

"You can thank the good Lord they're too young for the war. One of my sons . . . well, he didn't make it through."

I was instantly sorry to have reminded Mr. Dobson of his loss and almost wished I'd left my sons at home. I looked down at their three little grins and realized how fortunate I was.

The cashier glanced at my little slip of paper and wrote a check for $7.31. Elmer brought us eighty-seven cents.

We had dinner that evening with Nat and his wife. My husband ceremoniously counted out forty-three cents and five mills as Nat's share of the proceeds.

"Elmer must be dead by now," I said, almost crying. The four of us had a somber moment, then raised our glasses to Elmer and Maizie. This had been our worst failure on the farm, and Gene and I both felt depressed.

"Aw, try not to worry," said Nat. "I still have Elmer's pedigree papers. Some day those papers will be worth more to me than a whole herd of sheep."

"It's 'flock,' " Gene instructed, "at least according to the dictionary and the government bulletin."

We both knew Nat's opinion of the government. He and my husband often competed to see who could tell the most outrageous story about bureaucrats.

"Government bulletin?" asked Nat. "You tried to raise Elmer and his harem with a government bulletin?"

"Well, yes," confessed my husband. "But I'll never try that again."

"In that case," said Nat generously, "Elmer's life hasn't been wasted."

FIVE

THE
HOME FRONT

ightfoot was Gene's pride and joy. Even the Little Red Hussy took second place.

During the Depression, polo was not the rich man's sport it is today. Gene became addicted during his late teens. He spent years working out his own private formula for producing the perfect polo pony. Under his supervision, Lightfoot had been bred and foaled on the Verdigris farm — before the county took it over. Her sire was a standard American Thoroughbred racing horse, and her dam was half range bronco and half Hambletonian. Gene's theory was that the Thoroughbred would produce a long, supple neck and speed, the Hambletonian would produce stamina, and the bronco, spirit.

Lightfoot was only a halter-broken yearling when the county seized the Verdigris farm. Gene found a nearby rancher and rodeo performer, Bronc Wofford, and worked out a deal — Bronc would train Lightfoot with the understanding that he could use her on the ranch and in rodeos until Gene could take her back.

Bronc immediately trained Lightfoot for rodeo work and as a cutting horse. At a rodeo, the rider and the horse share the prize.

Bronc arranged with several riders to lease Lightfoot for a share of the prize money. With this method, she received a tremendous variety of training under a diversity of excellent riders.

Work as a cutting horse is similar to rodeo work. A cutting horse is trained to cut out specific animals from a herd of cattle. Lightfoot was unusually intelligent and picked up this more practical work in a matter of days.

By the time we were ready to bring Lightfoot to our farm, she was five years old and perfectly trained.

Lightfoot arrived in a one-horse trailer. I watched Gene back her out of the trailer — always a tricky moment. She was jittery after the long drive from north Tulsa County, and she had never been on our farm before. Although she could back up better than any horse I had ever seen, backwards is not a natural direction for a horse to move.

Lightfoot performed beautifully. She did not try to rear or run away, but let out a spirited whinny and tossed her handsome head. I fell in love with her on the spot. Her coat glistened a dark reddish brown. Her mane and tail were heavy and full, almost black.

A week passed before I was allowed to ride her, for Gene wanted Lightfoot to become completely familiar with her new home. In anticipation of Lightfoot's arrival, I visited the fanciest western store in Tulsa and purchased a pair of Pendleton riding pants, high-heeled western boots, and a brightly colored Indian beaded belt. I mean, I was ready!

My riding experience, however, was very limited. Gene told me that after three falls I would become a good rider. Of course, he never told me about any of his tumbles. He had seen me fall off a horse — my one and only fall — about two years earlier. I'd mounted a horse at a friend's ranch and simply was not prepared. The horse stepped forward too quickly, and I tumbled off backwards. Not much of a fall, but very embarrassing.

As soon as Lightfoot became acclimated to our terrain, I — the "intrepid horsewoman," as Gene was beginning to say with monotonous repetition — was finally allowed to ride.

I put my left foot in the stirrup and swung myself up, with the silent approval of my observing husband. There I was, astride Lightfoot, still as a statue. I gave the reins the tiniest shake and wriggled my boots just slightly against her lean flanks.

Zoom! Lightfoot sped off like a flash. She was a rodeo horse who could cut to perfection as well as carry a polo player anywhere on the field — but only at top speed. Why move out unless you wanted to get there pronto?

But that didn't fool me — this time I was prepared. I did not tumble over backwards. Lightfoot's speed, however, was frightening. I wanted her to stop, so I yelled, "Stop!" but to no avail. And there were no brakes anywhere. Silly me, I thought, I have to pull back on the reins. So I pulled back and reached for the saddle horn with both hands.

Lightfoot got the message and she stopped — on a dime. I was thrown forward onto her neck. I clutched at hunks of her mane in a supreme effort to avoid flying right over her beautiful head.

Lightfoot stood absolutely still, patiently waiting for me to recover and make my next move. After my breath returned, I felt a tremendous thrill.

I eased Lightfoot forward again. We turned, running at top speed, back towards Gene. Just short of him, I reined Lightfoot to the right. Trained as a cutting horse, Lightfoot naturally made a ninety-degree right turn. To my chagrin, I kept moving forward — straight out into thin air — and plopped down in an ungraceful heap ten feet from my husband. The moment he saw I was not hurt, he smiled, saying, "That's number two."

Lightfoot stopped the moment I tumbled off and obediently waited for me to get up. What a beauty she was! In those exhilarating few seconds, I'd learned more about horseback riding than I had in the previous three years.

Gene decided my next lesson should be separating animals. We were grazing a small herd of cattle at the bottom of our rocky hill where the grass grew. I mounted Lightfoot and Gene waved his hand, saying, "Choose any animal."

Such simple instructions seemed terribly vague. I eased Lightfoot into the herd and somehow designated a calf. Lightfoot plunged toward that calf like a dog after a rat. She could half-step from one side to another and then move forward so quickly I could hardly keep my balance. I clutched the reins and the saddle horn and hoped for the best.

Once Lightfoot separated the calf from the herd, she forced the animal back into a fence corner and stayed there until I reined her away. I was totally fascinated. Gene had never told me that horses could be so accomplished, but I knew Lightfoot was exceptional.

The romance that permeated the world of horses held a strong grip on me from that day forward. Tending and currying Lightfoot, then saddling and riding her were special joys in our busy farm life. Then my husband announced his plan.

"The plan," he explained, "is a colt for each son."

Lightfoot was in season, ready to be bred. The breeding period for mares lasts only days. Gene was in a hectic phase at the factory and often worked fourteen hours a day. On the better days, including Saturday and Sunday, he was gone only twelve hours. Ten-hour days were a faint and pleasant memory.

Gene was unusually indecisive. He kept asking, "We want that colt, don't we?"

Sure, I kept agreeing.

"Okay —" and he looked at me in a rather odd way, "you . . . ah . . . you'll have to take care of it."

Getting a mare bred might be a new one for me, but these war times meant a lot of new things. So I innocently said I would take care of Lightfoot.

Early the following morning I carried a gallon of milk to the Wilsons'. Their cow had just dried up, and we often traded to keep everyone in fresh milk. Myrtie welcomed me, as always, with a cup of rich, strong coffee full of cream and sugar. She lived on the stuff.

"Lightfoot's ready for breeding," I said. "My husband is swamped with work. Do you know where I can find a stud? We were thinking about a palomino —"

"Honey, I don't know nothin' about breeding horses, and I don't want to know. That's man's business. I ain't never heard of a woman gettin' involved."

"But the war's on," I said. "I've got to get Lightfoot bred."

"Wait till the goddamned war is over, honey."

Myrtie's advice jolted me — but only a little. Gene hadn't told me about horse breeding being a man's business. I noticed there were a lot of little things like that he neglected to tell me — he just let me find out on my own. I had survived carting those dumb sheep to the stockyards. After that, breeding Lightfoot seemed easy.

From Myrtie's I drove to a small dry-goods store. Shoe stamps had just arrived in the mail, and I wanted to outfit the boys in new and bigger shoes. The owner of the store, Brad Goodson, had been a friend since high school days. Brad had recently plunged into the quarter horse business and could talk of nothing else. In fact, he had shown me the first check he had received from selling a horse. Suddenly, I knew Brad was the man to help me in my problem. First I explained that my husband was swamped with work. Then I mentioned Lightfoot's delicate condition. Where, I asked blithely, could I find a palomino stud?

Brad was a very honest and straightforward person. He stood very still and looked at me kind of funny. What was wrong with everyone? Breeding a horse surely wasn't that big a deal. But I knew something was tinkling around inside his head. Finally he said, "Believe it or not, I've got just the man for you right over there."

There wasn't a real cracker barrel in the corner, but a group of men were gathered, talking and laughing. Brad introduced me to Josh — a small, wiry man who looked all cowboy.

"Yep," he said, kind of slow and puzzled. "I got me a fine palomino stud. Name of Silver. But I don't have no horse trailer."

"I . . . could rent one."

"'Kay. I live up Turley way. I kin draw you a map."

I agreed to a one o'clock meeting at his farm with a trailer in tow.

I rushed home to feed the boys lunch, then got back into the car with my sons, and off we drove to a trailer rental place. The attendant, an older man, hitched me up as if I had been to his place a dozen times. I paid the necessary fee and drove off nervously since I'd never towed a trailer before. The steering wheel jerked in my hand, and I kept expecting the trailer to sail off into a ditch. But gradually I began to get the hang of that wriggling load behind my car.

I lurched on out to Josh's farm and pulled up to the gate. His tough, wiry frame sprinted out of the farmhouse. Leaving the boys in the front seat, I tried to be casual and nonchalant — as if I were on an ordinary, everyday sort of errand. But all the time I was beginning to wonder just what my husband had gotten me into.

Josh gave a whistle and over the hill bounded Silver. I had never before been so close to a stallion, and Silver was an awesome animal. His coat was a silvery gold that glinted brightly in the hot sun. He had a long, white, silky mane that fell over his huge eyes. His neck arched perfectly, and he swung his head up and down in an impatient, spirited way while his long silvery tail swished from side to side.

What a colt Lightfoot would produce with this gorgeous creature!

Silver was beautifully trained despite his spirited prancing, and Josh soon had him loaded into the horse trailer. After closing the gate, Josh joined me and my sons in the car. I started driving — and immediately was aware of 1,500 pounds of restless horseflesh behind me. The car bucked and swayed, but nothing could faze me now.

We drove to our farm, and I pulled as close as I could to the corral where we kept Lightfoot. All at once our sweet, gentle mare went crazy. She raced around and around the corral, kicked up her heels, and whinnied and neighed like I had never heard before. I stood there, amazed and even a little embarrassed by Lightfoot's behavior.

Josh's face never changed expression. He backed Silver out of the trailer. This magnificent stallion was trembling, but Josh still had him under firm control. I waited, knowing vaguely what was going to happen, but not sure what the next step would be.

"You can hold Silver, can't you?" asked Josh abruptly.

Me? Me hold this gigantic palomino that was pawing the ground and tossing his enormous head high in the air right over me?

"S-s-sure," I said unsteadily. Josh gave me Silver's reins. I expected to be thrown down and dragged into the corral, but to my amazement, Silver simply stood still, although he continued pawing the ground with his powerful front hooves. All I could see was that gorgeous head bobbing up and down and the wild look in those great eyes.

Josh quickly caught Lightfoot and led her into our small barn with its Dutch-style half door. He returned to report that Lightfoot was ready. I hardly needed that information after seeing the way she had been cavorting. Josh took Silver's reins, muttering that he would, of course, need my assistance. "Oh, sure," I said, without the slightest idea what I was supposed to do. I was beyond clear thinking and was reduced to merely reacting when Josh indicated he wanted something. He now proceeded to parade Silver back and forth in front of Lightfoot. I watched, fascinated, as these two increasingly passionate animals began rolling their eyes at each other.

Suddenly, I noticed my sons. I had literally forgotten them. There they stood, glued to the fence of the corral. Three pairs of round, young, innocent eyes were widening with curiosity and wonderment. "Mother," asked one boy, "what is that yellow horse going to do with that great big penis?"

I glanced around in utter confusion. My God, this was not exactly the right moment for an intimate mother-child talk concerning the sex life of horses! The children were making Josh nervous at a very crucial time for Silver and Lightfoot. "Could you send them up to the house?" he suggested.

"Boys," I said in a firm though very strained voice, "Mother's busy. I'll explain everything later. *Now get back up to the house!*" I pointed vaguely and immediately turned around, ready to perform my next duty, whatever that might be.

I was so preoccupied I never knew whether the boys left or stayed. Josh had Lightfoot out of the barn, and I was needed. He handed Lightfoot's reins to me. For some reason I stepped onto a bale of hay. When I straightened up, I was looking right into Silver's eyes, just over Lightfoot's head. I will never forget those eyes. They seemed glazed in a soft, soulful way, while that silky white mane spilled over his forehead. If a horse can express sensual satisfaction, then Silver's eyes showed complete equine happiness.

It was all over in a matter of seconds. I released Lightfoot's reins, and Josh promptly led Silver back to the trailer. I had to find my sons. I started towards the house. They were halfway between the barn and the house, and I couldn't tell which way they were walking. At that point I didn't really care. "We're going in the car again," was all I could say. None of my three boys asked me any further questions —
ever.

Shudders of relief were beginning to flow over me. All I had to worry about now was the drive back to Josh's farm. Silver was quieter, and the steering wheel was steadier in my hands.

It was well into the afternoon, and the heat of the Oklahoma summer day was tremendous. As we skirted the edge of town, Josh, who had been silent for some time, spoke up. "Sure is hot. We could stop at that place up ahead for a beer."

That was exactly what I needed. We pulled in and ordered two frosty mugs of 3.2 percent, Oklahoma-approved beer and one whole soda for each boy. I seldom allowed the children carbonated soft drinks, so they were ecstatic. I can still remember their tiny hands clutching those big bottles. I had a feeling this had been a very special day for the three of them.

I delivered Josh and Silver to their farm, returned the trailer to the rental place, and headed for home. I was exhausted.

Lightfoot was back to normal, and I made certain she had fresh water. When Gene arrived home, I made a full report. He seemed satisfied with the whole transaction. Actually, thinking the experience over, I thought I'd handled the whole affair with flawless perfection. The war, I decided, was doing more than just changing the map of the world.

Naively, I assumed the episode of Lightfoot and Silver was over.

Two evenings later — with dinner finished and the boys asleep — I joined my husband, who was immersed in the evening paper. The quiet was disrupted with the jangling of the telephone. I answered. It was Josh. I could hear faint honky-tonk music in the background. Josh, in his easy way, asked me to join him at a beer hall. I tried to be nice — I started hedging, attempting to make some excuse. I looked over at my husband and noticed the newspaper rattling in a very odd manner. After I hung up, I discovered my husband was laughing. "Just a lonesome cowboy," he said through his ribald chortling.

My spun-out excuse over the phone must have sounded pretty weak, because Josh called me again the very next evening. His voice was slurred, and he sounded gentle but very persistent. This time I decided that politeness was inappropriate. I'd had all the guff I could stand from the male sex — of any animal. I was curt and to the point, and I concluded by slamming the receiver down as hard as I could.

Then I turned to my husband, still angry. "You got me into this! *Men* are supposed to be the horse breeders."

"Not anymore," replied Gene. "I think Lightfoot is pregnant — with foal, that is. Congratulations."

A beautiful palomino filly was the result. We called her Miss Honey. When we presented this elegant colt to our eldest son, he looked disappointed.

"But I wanted a bicycle," he said.

All I could think was — MEN!

Pigs are *snide*. They may be very intelligent, but they don't have a smidgen of sense about decent manners or even ordinary hygiene. I've never understood what people mean when they pointedly grin and say, "Pigs is pigs, you know." For my money, the brutes are sarcastic, greedy, and vicious.

My husband dealt in pigs for years. During our courtship I heard occasional reports: "The pig market is up" or "The pig market is down."

"Pigs are quick money," explained my husband. "I never lost a penny on any pig that didn't die."

I freely admit that I am afraid of pigs. They have substantial teeth and are not above sinking them into another pig, especially when quarreling over a juicy morsel of garbage. I've noticed that on occasion a pig will nip at a human being. More than their big teeth or even their ill humor, what really disturbs me is their intelligence. Occasionally I've seen a pig flop back his ears, raise his head, and stare right at me. Those bright, beady eyes look very accusing and very human. A pig as a biological organism is frighteningly similar to a human being. Perhaps that was George Orwell's reason for casting them as dictators in *Animal Farm*.

Gene was always "in pigs" with someone else. On our farm, Wee Willy Wilson became his staunch partner. The Wilsons' plot of land was only five acres. They usually had a pig or two fattening for their personal use. But on our farm the two men had a productive, paying pig business going all year round. Pig money financed everything from Lightfoot, the Little Red Hussy, the barns, and feed for the milk cows to taxes. If we had been in pure pigs, I think we might have made a profit on the farm. I didn't like pigs on a personal basis, but as instruments of profit, I grudgingly admit they saved us from disaster on more than one occasion.

The pigpen was off in a corner of our farm far away from the cowshed and horse barn. With Wee Willy on hand, the pigs were one chore I usually didn't have to worry about. All I saw was a truckload of big, grunting hogs going off to market or perhaps a load of squealing young shoats coming in. Sometimes a sow would eat a couple of her litter, and there would be general consternation all around. How disgusting to realize pigs would cannibalize their own kind!

Pigs require constant attention — which means a lot to eat. Gene was always bringing home odd lots of food in the pickup. One day he arrived with a thousand loaves of bread. My curiosity led me right down to the pigpen. He and Willy were tearing off wrappers.

"Where did you get that quantity of bread?" I asked.

"It's day-old bread from a big commercial bakery," explained my husband. "A penny a loaf. Only ten dollars for this whole load."

"What a bargain!" I remarked sarcastically.

Wilson soaked each loaf in a bucket of skimmed milk, then threw the squashy bundles to the pigs. Wow, did they scramble for that mess! The brutes fought snout to snout until Wilson pushed a soggy loaf in front of each animal.

Late one August, Gene turned up with a hundred watermelons. He and Wilson dropped each melon on a rock to break it open. I stood by to collect the juicy, seedless hearts. Then we tossed the remainder to the pigs. There is little food value in watermelons, but the pigs loved gorging themselves on anything we threw to them. We, in turn, stuffed ourselves for days.

With the war going full tilt and "You take care of it" the order of the day, I eventually found myself in the pig business. One day after feeding those animals, I noticed that the garbage never stayed in the trough. So why put it there? Instead I tossed the garbage *at* the pigs. They never seemed to mind. A pig would nibble a bit of mashed potato off another pig's ear as willingly as out of the trough.

One morning Willy Wilson knocked on the door. "Sorry to bother you, ma'am, but one of the pigs has come down with diarrhea. Got any Kaopectate in the house?"

I had an old bottle almost full. Down I trotted to the pigpen, bottle in hand. A middling-sized pig weighing about a hundred pounds was looking puny and sad.

Wilson stepped over the low fence and beckoned me to follow. I did, reluctantly, and for the first time came face to face with a dozen unsmiling, grim-faced pigs. Wilson could just about pass for a pig himself, given his short, rotund stature. His gray overalls camouflaged him well. But I was in riding pants and a yellow blouse — the wrong color, I was sure.

Wilson walked right up to the ailing pig, grabbed his leg, and flipped him over on his back. The squeal was piercing, but Wilson outweighed this porker by more than a hundred pounds.

"Now pour!" shouted Wilson over the squeals.

I uncapped the bottle of Kaopectate and poured a little of the chalky stuff into the pig's upside-down mouth. The squeal abruptly became a fierce protesting gurgle.

"More!" hollered Wilson. I poured more. The gurgling became a high-pitched gargle. I kept pouring. In fact, I poured the whole bottle into that gaping mouth. The beleaguered pig managed to spit out a lot, but some of the medicine slid down his gullet.

Wilson let go. The pig bounded to his feet, and I backed toward the fence, expecting an attack. The pig stood there giving me a beady glare, then walked over to the water trough and drank deeply.

A week later, Wilson pronounced the pig greatly improved. Together, Wilson and I had saved a vet's fee — and possibly a pig's life. I felt like a porcine Florence Nightingale.

That pack of pigs was sold, and the two men purchased another dozen young shoats.

A day later Wilson knocked on the door again. By this time, my reputation as a horse breeder was well established and the general rumor in the neighborhood was that I would tackle anything. "Ma'am, there's seven of them shoats that needs castrating."

"You'll have to wait for my husband," I said firmly. It wasn't that I was squeamish. At least twenty times I had seen Myrtie grab a chicken by the head, give it a whirl, then a yank. The head remained in her hand, while the body ran off a few yards before expiring. Myrtie always claimed she was scared of an ax. Twisting off a chicken's head by hand was not for me, but on more than one occasion I'd put the ax to a chicken so I could get on with dinner. However, performing surgery on several male pigs was simply beyond me, war or no war.

Gene arrived home late in the evening. The sun had set, so there was no light at the pigpen. Wilson appeared. My husband started sharpening his knife. "We need you to hold the lantern," he said.

"Can't you tie it to a fence post or something?" I asked.

"Pigs squirm around," he said. "Wilson or I could step into the light. Our lantern isn't very heavy."

I thought of a dozen reasons why I shouldn't be included. All fell flat. I finally agreed to hold the lantern, rationalizing that this was my contribution to the war effort.

We headed down to the pigpen. Gene pumped up the gasoline lantern until it threw out a brilliant glow and handed it to me. The new pigs were uneasy. They knew something was up, and none of them liked this evening intrusion.

Wilson grabbed a thirty-pounder and threw him into an empty trough. Gene made the incision quickly, extracted the testicle, and cut the cord. Then he painted a tar-like antiseptic on the incision. He made another incision . . . on and on fourteen times. I was counting unsteadily.

I finally became numb and just tried my best to hold the lantern where the men wanted light. The squeals were like nothing I had ever heard before. But at least each operation was quick.

After the last animal had endured his operation, the pigs quieted down rather quickly. They even started nosing around for scraps of garbage. What a relief to have those screams over with.

"Here," said my husband with a mischievous grin. "Dinner meat for tomorrow night." He handed me a pie pan full of slippery pigs' testicles. I'd heard of mountain oysters before, but *hearing* was as close as I wanted to get.

"Dip 'em in milk and eggs, then in flour," said Wilson. "Then fry 'em up good."

"You take them," I said.

"Why, thankee, ma'am. Myrtie just loves oysters."

I was so glad. My husband was a little disappointed that I'd chickened out. But I explained that we had plenty of meat, since we were raising most of it ourselves. I could hardly wait for this war to be over. When they signed the peace treaty I was never going near a pigpen again.

World War II drew the country together in a unique way. Still, moments of doubt led to some grumbling with the inconveniences of rationing, which quickly became our way of life. There was a feeling that the war was "over there" and we were fighting as much for somebody else as for our own country. My philosophy was to turn these difficulties into a game. I purchased all of our groceries from one source, and as a result, the butcher and I became good friends. When certain choice items arrived, he would save them for me. I felt slightly wicked, but I was determined to feed my family well.

Through Pathé News, radio, and the newspapers, the U.S. military strategy became clearer and more exciting. Slowly we began to understand the fighting all around the world. The most striking evidence of the war to us personally was the construction of the Douglas Aircraft factory two miles from our farm. This long, low building changed our prairie view dramatically. The factory was camouflaged in green and brown, but from our hilltop the outline of the building was extremely obvious. I doubted that any German or Japanese spies would make it this far inland, but I felt certain some paint contractor was cashing in his chips. As that building and others like it were built, thousands and thousands of workers were hired, bringing middle America into the war.

The standing comment about the huge Douglas plant was that, with so many thousands of men and women working there and with so many millions of dollars' worth of high-grade supplies disappearing into that long building, an airplane simply had to pop out every so often.

Over at the Spartan factory, Gene was becoming the expert in obtaining necessary and hard-to-get materials. There was a constant hassle even though every regulation showed he was entitled to the parts and materials he was attempting to obtain.

Early one morning Gene called me, explaining that he would be flying in a Spartan company plane to St. Louis where he would pick up 300 pounds of counterweights the workers needed *right now*. The counterweights were stuck in St. Louis and could proceed no further without personal intervention. Gene assured me he would be home for dinner.

Three days later he appeared in a rumpled suit and wrinkled shirt with a borrowed toothbrush in his pocket. His story of bureaucratic ineptitude topped all he had been through before.

Gene and his pilot flew in a Spartan Executive, a handsome, sleek single-engine airplane manufactured before the war started. The Spartan Executive had a piston engine that included two magnetos. They flew to St. Louis successfully, loaded the counterweights, and took off for the return trip. One magneto promptly quit. Even though there was an extra magneto, this was an emergency of frightening proportions. My husband was constantly lecturing about one thing or another, and one of his favorites was, "In a piston-driven engine, ignition plus fuel plus compression equals power." There they were, sailing through the air with just one of those magnetos, which meant they were dangerously low on ignition. If the second magneto stopped working, they would fall out of the sky.

The pilot tossed a map at my husband, and together they decided the nearest landing field was an Army/Air Force base in Missouri.

Dropping in on this base may have been an easy decision for the two men, but personnel on the ground regarded their arrival from an entirely different viewpoint. After the pilot established radio contact, the air controller on the ground caustically cited AAF regulations that did not permit the landing of civilian aircraft. Gene ordered the pilot to turn off his radio and proceed to land. As the pilot approached the airfield, my husband calmly watched as several flashing red beacons warned them not to land. A jeep and truck full of armed soldiers appeared on the runway. The pilot looked at Gene for instructions. Gene managed a forced smile, saying, "I think they are on our side."

They landed. The jeep roared up to the plane and out stepped the officer of the day, a very young second lieutenant. Despite vigorous efforts to keep the Spartan plane from landing, the lieutenant was amazingly congenial. This was no doubt the first excitement he had encountered since entering the AAF. Gene explained the magneto problem, then rattled off a speech about how important the counterweights were. Apparently these counterweights would be part of the mechanism for the wing- and tail-control surfaces in a huge new aircraft designed for the invasion of Japan.

The commanding officer of the base was called and quickly appeared. Gene repeated his speech, and the CO seemed favorably impressed. In fact, he assured my husband that he would do all he could to help.

Gene was given accommodations in the visiting officers' barracks, a razor, and a toothbrush. By the time the Spartan Executive was fixed the following morning, fog and a misty rain had closed the runways. Gene was now extremely concerned about keeping the Spartan factory on schedule. The commanding officer again offered his assistance. The two men loaded the 300 pounds of counterweights in the officer's personal car and drove to the nearest railroad crossing. There they flagged the next train, but the railroad people, operating under strict government regulations, refused to load the counterweights. As soon as the regulations were thrown in his face, Gene declared the weights as personal baggage. Finally the two men muscled the weights on board the train.

Unfortunately the Santa Fe line which they'd flagged didn't go all the way to Tulsa. This meant Gene would have to transfer himself and his "personal baggage" to the Frisco line. When he attempted to make the transfer, he was curtly informed that 300 pounds of aircraft hardware could not be passed off as personal baggage. Railway Express forms had to be filled out in detail. The weights, as express freight, had to go into Kansas City and be transferred again.

Gene was furious, but determined to get those counterweights to Tulsa. He demanded to see a copy of the railroad's regulations and studied them until he found a loophole. By paying an extra fee (out of his own pocket), he was able to designate the routing. The railroad people were miffed but could do nothing to stop the transaction.

Off the train rolled, Gene in a coach, the weights in the express car. Each time the train stopped, Gene hopped out of the coach, ran to the express car, and argued with the freight handlers to keep them from unloading the counterweights.

Finally, Gene and the weights arrived in Tulsa. For reasons never clear, the handlers did not want to unload the counterweights. A Spartan truck pulled up beside the freight car, and Gene spoke quickly to the driver, "We'll unload the weights ourselves."

"You're not supposed to do the unloading," complained a railroad employee.

"Go check with your supervisor," demanded Gene. The moment the railroad man was gone, Gene signaled to the truck driver. Both men jumped into the express car and unloaded the weights. Gene signed the receipt and stuck the paper in the door handle.

The supervisor was just huffing up as they drove away. "See you at the next world war," waved my husband. "That is, if both of us live that long."

After a hot shower and dinner, Gene slept solidly for ten hours. The battle on the factory floor would ultimately be won — not because of helpful government regulations, but because individual men over our entire country were willing to work their way through and around bureaucratic red tape. Those men didn't win a Silver Star or a glamour spot on Pathé News, but at least I knew my husband's perseverance made a difference.

When "we" became pregnant the first time, Gene and I felt the need for written guidance. No one had come up with the idea of giving classes to inexperienced parents-to-be. We were overwhelmed with mother and mother-in-law advice, mothers contradicting mothers-in-law as often as not. Surely there was positive assistance somewhere!

The United States government came to our aid — I could almost hear the trumpets blaring as the cavalry charged over the hill. We discovered that many departments published *free* bulletins. To my amusement, the Labor Department issued bulletins on being pregnant, the baby's first few days at home, how to nurse a child (few doctors at that time encouraged such a primitive practice), and even how to keep from having another child immediately. All these bulletins were well written and filled with excellent advice. One phrase was repeated on each page — *Parents Must Work Together.*

Those first bulletins so impressed us that, as the farm became a reality, we began ordering bulletins from the Agriculture Department. We found that there were hundreds available just for the asking. My desk contained a reference collection that would have rivaled that of any Oklahoma agricultural college. Both of us were becoming experts on farrowing houses, milking barns, vegetable canning, meat curing, sausage making, hog butchering, soil conservation, stockpond excavation, septic-tank cleaning, animal breeding, head-crop planting, berry cultivation, butter making, cottage-cheese culturing, and storm-cellar construction.

We collected three assortments of animals — those we purchased, those reproduced on our farm, and those that got lost and found us. The road still ended at our farm, providing us with an amazing variety of wandering animals, much to the delight of our sons. Several dogs arrived, and we fed and petted them all.

Twice each week a flock of turkeys — a huge tom with a dozen hens — marched through our yard. They gobbled constantly, circled through our front yard eating everything they could get their beaks into, then disappeared over the hill. I was all for borrowing Myrtie's .22 rifle and bagging one for Thanksgiving dinner, but my husband said no.

Occasionally a cow turned up in our front yard, and by evening the owner would arrive to pilot the animal home. I awakened one morning, musing, "Well, I wonder what I'll find in our front yard this morning." As I shuffled towards my kitchen, I peeked out the window. There stood four enormous mules! We had been working hard to scrape a yard together. Now we watched unbelievingly as the ugly quartet milled around trampling everything, bumping into each other, and fertilizing the grass.

"Do something, Gene!" I yelled.

Gene walked outside, looked thoughtfully at the mules and finally waved his hands. "Shoo!" he said. The mules stared at him briefly, but didn't move. They remained with us for two whole days. I thought I would lose my mind *and* my front yard. The owner finally arrived with a truck and, without a single word to me, loaded the beasts and — thank heavens — drove away forever.

Two weeks later, a pretty little spotted calf appeared. We enticed her into our corral to keep her until the owner made his claim. The boys fell in love with her, for she had a sweet disposition and loved attention. They began to pet and feed her special bits of grain. She followed them around like a puppy.

The calf had been with us three weeks when a couple brought their fourteen-year-old daughter Karen to see our farm. The boys could hardly wait to show Karen our new calf that had just "appeared." They danced around the calf extolling her virtues. "We're going to name our calf Karen!" they sang. "Just like you!" The real Karen was not too happy about a calf having her name, especially when our sons kept pushing the animal towards her for her to pet. The boys babbled away about their Karen's future — there would be a baptism with special feed. The human Karen backed off and headed for her parents' car where she remained until the end of the visit.

Karen the calf was petted and stuffed with all kinds of goodies. Still no one came for her. She grew plump with all the coddling, and my husband began to eye her for butchering. Karen would provide us with six months of practically free beef, he said. Finally Gene called Willy. In half an afternoon Karen was reduced to a fur rug, hamburger, steaks, ribs, roasts, and several gallons of blood and guts that were thrown away since we had no facilities for making glue. The children cried in great protest over this indignity to Karen. When they sat down to dinner, they wanted to know if the meat loaf was Karen. I explained carefully that we needed leather for shoes and belts, and meat to keep us strong. I considered my explanation supremely rational and I hope I assuaged their grief. To be honest, though, I myself could hardly eat that meat loaf. From this experience I learned you could create a minor god merely by giving something — anything — a name.

Still, we were willing to tackle anything with a government bulletin in hand. We built a rabbit hutch following a diagram, then purchased two beautiful white rabbits. The boys were ecstatic.

I then decided to raise six adorable baby ducklings right in my kitchen. We laughed over their constantly twitching little yellow tails. When they seemed grown enough to take on the outside world, we put them in a small pen near the house. That night a violent prairie storm blew in and drowned all six ducklings. For several hours, I thought my sons were going to perform a real funeral.

The rabbits survived the storm, however, and we had hopes for baby rabbits. But our two rabbits just sat in their hutch and looked at each other, twitching their noses and eating. I reread the rabbit bulletin, but all I could do was wait for nature to take its course. Still nothing happened. I felt cheated. All my life I'd heard that rabbits were supposed to breed . . . like rabbits. Finally we gave up and ate both rabbits smothered in gravy with hot biscuits. The boys never complained about eating the rabbits. In fact I think they were glad to get them out of the hutch; they immediately converted it to a prison for a dozen terrapins. I was afraid they would all starve, so one night I released the whole bunch. The only alternative would have been to make terrapin soup for which I had no recipe.

Relaxation for my husband was riding the Little Red Hussy. Every weekend possible he worked on our "yard." He stuck a hose in the center of the dry hole and ran water day and night attempting to wash away the salt damage. Finally he decided we had to get rid of that hole. We put every loose piece of farm debris we could find down that hole, and the hole ate it all — rocks, boulders, dirt from digging the storm cellar, an old dead tree from the pasture, and decaying fence posts. The little tractor did her bit — plowing, disking, and raking the ground. She must have loved those times with three boys climbing all over her, or Gene happily driving her, holding one or two boys on his lap.

I took my recreation in the milk shed — a cozy spot despite no heat. Here I bubbled home brew and wine, separated cream, and washed clothes. The aromas were pungent. I had a fine electric washing machine with a wringer and two tubs. I purchased big bars of washing soap and with a sharp knife sliced bits of soap into hot water. In ten minutes, suds formed, and I slung in the first batch of clothes. The challenge was to see how many sets of clothes I could wash with a single sudsing. We had a dandy solar-energy dryer — known in those days as a clothesline. On a beautiful sunny day, it was a joy to hang out wet clothes. But when the Oklahoma winds blew — which was most of the time — wet sheets whipped around me and twisted into flapping knots on the clothesline wires.

I took up jogging long before this form of exercise became the *in* thing. From my kitchen — the starting point — I raced through the porch, into the garage, around the corner, and into the milk shed. I threw in the second wash, checked my cream, then jogged the same course backwards. No fancy jogging suits in those days — if it was cold outside and I forgot my sweater, I just jogged a little faster. I was beginning to feel like one of the prairie roadrunners that dashed so swiftly over our rocks and through our fences. I had a flat stomach, rosy complexion, and messy, curly hair thanks to all those rural aerobics.

Every four months we waited for the mail with the card that updated Gene's draft status. My husband made himself invaluable at the defense plant, which meant longer and longer hours. I joked about his going "off to the war" every morning, but I was really very grateful he was home every night, spared the horrors of the shooting war overseas. We had lost personal friends on the African desert and at Salerno. I would have had few sympathizers had it occurred to me to complain about my chores.

We enjoyed and loved our funny lopsided house, especially the winter evenings in front of our huge fireplace. Gene would bank the red coals with ashes so that the next morning, fresh logs caught fire immediately. We were grateful to be together with our sons and prayed each evening for the end of this world debacle.

SIX

BIG RED, SWEET BETSY, AND BILL THE BULL

My husband didn't come to cows as an experienced farmhand — he was strictly a city boy. So when he acquired his first cow, Big Red, in 1941, he wasn't quite sure what to do.

He turned to a government bulletin. From the intensity of his study, I thought he was reading Aristotle's *Metaphysics*. The government insisted that cows be contented. So my husband led Big Red into our tiny barn and checked her for ticks, scratches, and mud. No ticks. He dabbed salve on one little barbed-wire scratch; with warm water he scrubbed mud off her udder. Then he gave her a double handful of feed. Okay, so Big Red was now content. What next?

My husband placed a three-legged stool he had made near the udder. He put a brand-new Sears galvanized-steel milk pail underneath. He was now as keyed up as he'd been just before taking his bar exams. With the government bulletin shaking in one hand, he approached Big Red. After a couple of false starts, he soon got a firm handle on the gentle art of milking a cow. We had gallons of fresh milk for the duration of the war.

Milk! If bread is the staff and meat our feast, then surely milk is what our cup runneth over with. We gorged ourselves on strawberries smothered in the thickest of cream. I started making butter using my electric mixer. That chore was too heavy for the motor; it burned out and had to be sent out of town for repair. I then resorted to the old-time method of the wooden butter churn operated by hand. I'll admit it was an unpleasant chore. It wasn't the muscle power that bothered me — it was just so damned boring pumping that thing up and down day after day after day.

I think back-to-the-basics is great, but the day we bought an electric Daisy churn was the day I experienced a quantum jump upward in my standard of living. You could actually see the cream turning to butter inside the big glass jar. My boys loved to watch it, and so did I.

One late Sunday afternoon Betsy appeared in our front yard. She was leading my husband by a rope. I don't know where he found her — probably at the end of a rainbow, to hear him talk about it.

Betsy was a Jersey cow with a muted beige coat and soft brown eyes. My husband thought she was the perfect embodiment of femininity. She was smaller than most cows, very well shaped, shy, and good tempered. I had to listen to an exhaustive list of her virtues, from her tiny little horns to the tip of her swishing tail. She had an enormous udder that gave vast quantities of luscious rich milk. The cream was so thick it wouldn't pour — you had to spoon it.

While my husband would allow anyone to feast his eyes on Betsy for any length of time, *no one* but himself was allowed to touch her. The only exception to this strict rule was that if Gene was unavoidably detained out of town, I was to call in Willy Wilson. A cow can miss one milking, but not two.

Though we loved Betsy best, we did venture a little farther into the cattle business. Forty acres is hardly a vast spread, especially where there's only a teacup of rain each month, but our farm did give us the opportunity to run a few head of cattle. Our entire herd was never larger than twelve — mostly beef cattle — but that gave us all the meat we could eat plus an extra animal to sell now and then.

When our milk-cow population got up to four, my husband realized that if we bought a bull, we could start producing calves and make some real money. But good bulls cost money — a lot of money.

New Year's Eve was in the offing, and we decided to have a party. In addition to our usual crowd of city friends and business associates, there were two other couples my husband wanted me to invite. The first couple was Polly and Frank Heddlestone.

"But we haven't seen them since the day we moved out here," I protested.

"This war can't last forever," said my husband. "When it's over, Frank could be a valuable business contact for me."

"And Polly is part of the bargain?" I asked.

"Polly and Frank," he sighed, "come as a package."

Actually it was great fun seeing them again. Frank was his usual cool, successful self. Polly hadn't mellowed; in fact, she looked like a nervous wreck, but she rattled on and on about our farm. She couldn't seem to see enough. They came out early, while it was still light, and among other delights my husband showed them Betsy.

Other guests began to arrive, including a new couple, Ritchie and Susanna Foss.

Not long before, Ritchie Foss had applied for a job at Spartan and had gone to work for my husband. Before the war he went from job to job as a supersalesman. He was one of the most gifted men on a telephone my husband and I had ever known. While Spartan didn't need salesmen in the usual sense, Ritchie Foss's communication talents were quickly put to use. In the back of everyone's mind was what could happen when the war was over. Then a supersalesman such as Ritchie Foss would be needed at Spartan.

I met Ritchie's wife, Susanna Foss, and before long we discovered that we were distantly related through some southern roots. Susanna had an incredible mind and would have made a terrific trial lawyer.

Ritchie and Susanna, despite their talents, were not perfect diamonds. She was a big, abrasive woman, and he ate, drank, and smoked compulsively. One of the first things I learned about Ritchie was that he didn't like children — neither his own nor mine. This always made me uneasy.

But here they were at our New Year's Eve celebration — and they were terrific party people. Everyone was enjoying the fact that we'd recently acquired an entire case of fine bootleg Scotch. After we'd exhausted the usual topics — the war, business, the current gossip — the conversation inevitably shifted to life on our farm. Ordinary happenings for us became exciting, exotic tales for our guests. Finally, my husband was unable to resist bringing up Betsy. His eulogy was so impassioned that I thought she'd just died.

Polly Heddlestone finally asked the question: "But . . . how do you milk a cow?" I knew my husband had been waiting for this one. This was his most highly polished performance.

"Hm, an interesting question, now that you mention it. Let me see . . . how can I demonstrate the milking of a cow?"

Polly was literally shaking with curiosity.

"Oh yes," said my calculating husband. "Polly, try this. Lace your fingers together. Good. Now turn the palms of your hands away from you — keeping your fingers laced."

Polly went through this minor contortion in a very cooperative fashion.

"Now you'll notice" he said, "that your two thumbs are hanging down — like two cow's tits."

"I thought they were called teats," objected Polly mildly.

"On a farm," he said, "they're tits. And a cow has four. But we'll demonstrate with just your two here."

My husband grasped Polly's two pendant thumbs as if he were going to milk.

"Now you don't just grab and squeeze," he said. "You must strip the milk gently, but firmly." And he proceeded to "milk" Polly's thumbs by tightening each of his fingers in rapid succession, from top to bottom. "A cow likes that," he said. "She'll let go of her milk for anyone who treats her right. Now Betsy —"

My husband was continuing to demonstrate. Polly's face suddenly turned bright red. She yanked her hands away from the demonstration and clutched them together in front of her. "That feels just like —" she wailed. Then she crumpled in embarrassment. She ran off to the bathroom in tears. Frank went after her.

Ritchie Foss had been leering his way through the whole scene. He was practically chugalugging straight Scotch. "Wow, that was some demonstration!" he said.

"Well, it never turned out quite like that before," said my properly embarrassed husband.

"Tell me more about Betsy," urged Ritchie. "She must be some cow."

The conversation lurched on about cattle all evening. Finally it came out that my husband wanted to buy a bull. But he needed a partner.

"I'll go in with you!" exclaimed Ritchie. "Seriously. I've got some extra money stashed away. I can't think of a better investment."

I watched, aghast, as my husband shook hands on the deal. Suddenly, we were in the cattle-breeding business.

Bill the Bull was no cheap animal. He weighed almost a ton, cost an arm and a leg, and came with papers. He was a registered Hereford — better known in Oklahoma as a "whiteface."

No mature bull is exactly friendly. A mild-tempered bull may tolerate humans, but there's never any affection. A mean bull is a threat to life. This meant a change in the pattern of our fences, gates, and pastures as well as in the distribution of animals. My husband's plan was to keep Bill the Bull in a pen and let him out only to breed. We had only one so-called corral. With a full-grown bull about to arrive, reinforcement was needed.

Ritchie Foss and Gene ordered oak planks and some extra-heavy fence wire. The oak was so tough that my husband had to dip each nail in a can of grease before he could drive it into the board. Ritchie stood by, drink in hand, watching and talking steadily. He was afraid to drive any nails himself for fear of bashing his fingers, but he threw himself into all the rest of the labor with heart-attack-inducing fervor. When any of his or our children came near he shooed them away. I wasn't too happy about that since a major reason we were on the farm was to expose the children to all facets of life. They were already picking up many of the physical abilities that my husband had developed painstakingly as an adult.

111

Bill the Bull arrived in the back of a two-ton truck. Ritchie Foss inspected him intimately, right there in the truck, then pronounced him to be "some fine bull all right." I looked at Bill the Bull too. He carried his head low, I thought. His eyes roved over us all without fear. He was calm, waiting to see what facilities we had to offer.

We unloaded him down the chute into the oak-reinforced double-wired bull pen. Would it hold him?

Bill the Bull strode majestically into the middle of his pen. He put his right foot forward and pawed the ground with a mighty heave. A solid piece of turf flew high into the air over his back.

"Jeez, lookit that!" said Ritchie.

Bill the Bull ambled over to the stock tank and drank deeply. He was obviously thirsty after his long truck ride. My husband was pleased. Bill the Bull was accepting our water — an important sign.

Ritchie poured himself another drink. He took a large handful of peanuts out of his pocket and nervously stuffed them in his mouth. "Okay, now. Looks great. Okay . . . when are we going to let him breed?"

"None of the cows is in season," said my husband.

"Oh." Ritchie was severely disappointed. More peanuts. A gulp of Scotch. "Okay, so like when maybe . . . ."

"I'll give you a call," offered my husband.

"Oh great! Great!"

My husband fed Bill the Bull carefully. Bill consumed bales and bales of our no-longer-virgin prairie hay, crumbled cottonseed cake softened in water, mineral supplement, and salt. I almost expected Gene to offer that animal vegetables off our dinner table. My husband never got in the pen with the bull, but he would sit on the fence to watch him eat. Now and then I saw Bill the Bull look up at my husband. They seemed just to stare at each other — man to man.

Presently Big Red came into season. My husband notified Ritchie at work. Ritchie and Susanna showed up Saturday morning for the mating.

"This calls for a drink," said Ritchie. My husband and I didn't want to be killjoys, but we both declined, at least until the day's business was done. Somebody had to manage this operation. Susanna opted for "just a little one."

112

Then we went out to the storm cellar. Our storm cellar was a concrete room, half underground, half above the surface. It had become a favorite play area for the children, and over the past couple of years the grass had covered the sloping sides, making a ramp to the cellar's roof. From there, one could see our main pasture. It was the perfect vantage point. Ritchie and Susanna climbed up there to wait for the display.

Bill the Bull was waiting too. His sense of smell was acute, and he knew even better than Ritchie the condition of Big Red.

My husband opened the gate of the bull pen, then quickly stepped out of the way. Bill the Bull charged out of the pen. Big Red, a Guernsey in her prime, was expecting him.

Then we heard an odd rumble and a loud, challenging bellow. Big Red's condition had wafted through the air across several pastures. An ordinary fence means little to a mature bull. Another powerful-looking whiteface bull, wearing a metal yoke, broke through our fence at the far end of the pasture.

I'd never seen this kind of yoke before. It was simply a large metal ring around the neck with two prongs, one above the neck, one below, designed to catch fence wire and keep the animal from getting through a fence.

Ha! This sex-charged ton of bull didn't go *through* the fence; he destroyed it, knocking down a post and breaking the wire.

"My God!" screamed Ritchie. "It's the enemy! It's a Japanese bull — no, no, a *German* bull!"

I couldn't help laughing despite my intense concern. My husband sprinted out of that pasture like a shot, leaped over the fence, and ran to the barn. He reappeared with two lassos.

"What are you going to do?" yelled Ritchie.

Bill the Bull and the yoked intruder had squared off. They were pawing the ground ferociously. I could hear the rush of their heavy breathing from fifty yards away.

In appearance the two animals were not evenly matched. Our bull was larger, but we were soon to learn that keeping him penned had been a mistake. This prevented him from roaming freely, and we had inadvertently weakened him. The intruder was a range animal, and his greater conditioning made up for his smaller size.

This meant, in effect, that the two animals were about evenly matched.

Suddenly the enemy bull charged. The two animals clashed horns, then the enemy bull pivoted and gave our Bill the Bull a terrible head butt in the gut. I could hear Bill exhale heavily.

Gene entered the pasture with those two fighting bulls. I felt a wave of fear. Visions of his gored and trampled body filled my mind. I yelled something, but I knew it was hopeless for me to interfere.

Ritchie set down his drink and descended from the storm cellar roof. He grabbed a ten-foot length of 2 x 4 and clambered over the fence. Susanna screamed incoherently at him. Ritchie tried to shush her, to no avail.

I looked at the two bulls and was astonished to see that Bill the Bull had jammed one of his horns into the yoke of the other whiteface, strangely immobilizing the enemy bull. Then I noticed that our bull seemed to be twisting his horn in a effort to tighten the yoke — and so cut off the enemy's windpipe! I could hardly believe Bill the Bull's intelligence. He knew he was outpowered by the other bull's vicious charges. Strategy and cunning were the only ways to overcome this fearsome intruder.

Ritchie was suddenly brave. He approached the two preoccupied bulls and gave the intruding bull a great whack with his 2 x 4.

"Take that!" I heard him yell. Then he quickly backed away.

The blow startled the animal into jerking back, unfortunately freeing his yoke from Bill the Bull's horn. All our bull could do was stand his ground. The intruder bull charged, but Bill the Bull braced himself and even lunged forward to smash the charge. Bill the Bull's superior weight paid off, and the intruder's charge failed to do more than jar him. But the enemy bull's quickness enabled him to swirl to the side, and I had to watch our bull take another gut-wrenching blow to his vulnerable side. I heard him grunt in agony, and my heart went out to him.

But Bill the Bull was still alert and strong. After delivering his vicious side attack, the enemy bull's yoke was exposed, and our bull once again jammed his horn in the ring and twisted. The enemy bull literally gasped for breath.

My husband advanced with lasso in hand. He was not an expert roper. He'd never gone in for rodeos, but in managing our own little herd over the years, he'd roped an occasional animal.

I could see Ritchie winding up with his 2 x 4, but my husband yelled, "Hold it!" The enemy bull's horns were now in the open, as Bill the Bull continued to tighten the yoke. On the very first toss my husband got one lasso around both the intruder's horns. I cheered, and so did Susanna and Ritchie.

Neither bull really noticed the rope. But my husband quickly backed off to the very end of it and held it taut. He held on for several agonizing minutes as he waited for the flux of the battle to bring the two combatants near a fence post. With knot-tying skill bred of necessity, my husband lashed the rope to the base of a fence post.

But what now? Within a minute or two, the intruder bull would let the rope go slack and then he'd be able to shake it loose. My husband took the other lasso and quickly threw it around the bull's horns. With two ropes, Gene had some control. He tied the second rope to another post, effectively immobilizing the enemy bull.

Bill the Bull certainly didn't seem to mind the turn of events. He was one exhausted animal. But our attention was still on the intruder. Two thin ropes can't hold a bull forever. Ritchie had dropped his 2 x 4 and had run to help Gene. Together, fence post by fence post, tying and untying, the two men maneuvered the bull towards the bull pen. Before long they had him inside.

"This," announced Ritchie, "calls for a drink." He pulled a flask out of his pocket and let the booze gurgle freely down his throat.

"You know," said my husband, "I think I'd like a nip too."

"Sure. I saved you at least a whole shot."

My husband and Ritchie left the pasture and made their way rather wearily towards us. We left Bill the Bull in the pasture with Big Red and the other cows. But poor Bill was spent. Big Red nuzzled him affectionately, but clearly he would have to recover his strength.

Boy, was I relieved! I was about to join everyone else in a little drink. My children and the Fosses' two kids had played together all morning and had joined Susanna and me on the storm cellar for the last half of the bullfight.

When Ritchie saw all five children excitedly reviewing and beginning to reenact the bullfight, he yelled at them to go away.

I lost my temper. Not only had Ritchie endangered my husband with his stupid 2 x 4, he was now telling *me* how to raise *my* children. I gave him a withering verbal blast designed to penetrate a booze-fogged brain. After concluding on a deeply moving note about the glories of agrarian life, I thought I could see some contriteness in Ritchie's face. All he could say was, "Well, at least they didn't see anything they shouldn't have."

Bill the Bull recovered, and Big Red became pregnant. Her gestation went well. But the night of the birth a rare, heavy storm rolled in, and the calf drowned in the mud and rain. It seemed as though we could have — and should have — done something. Big Red's gestation was a little shorter than we'd expected, and we were caught unprepared. Her calf was the only animal we'd lost since Maizie, but we regarded it as merely unfortunate — not some great tragedy. In addition to the sex education our children were receiving, they were seeing life and death in terms of the natural flow of events.

Betsy came in season next. My husband dutifully notified Ritchie, but he didn't show up. Bill the Bull was of no mind to wait, and we soon knew Betsy was pregnant because she refused Bill's advances after the second servicing.

Betsy's gestation seemed normal enough except that she swelled to gigantic proportions. My husband began to have second thoughts about breeding a large whiteface to a small Jersey.

My orders were strict. I was to watch over Betsy like a protective grandmother. "You take care of it" was no joking matter.

Nature took its course; Betsy was soon ready to deliver. The water broke, and I stood around waiting. There was nothing I could do. I knew that cows remained standing for delivery. Eventually the calf's head appeared, but nothing more. The calf, I finally realized, was too big. Betsy began to strain. She doubled up, still in a standing position, and pushed and pushed. Nothing happened. I couldn't imagine what I could possibly do. Finally I ran to the house and called Doc Pfeiffenhauser, our neighborhood veterinarian.

Doc Pfeiffenhauser had immigrated to the United States after World War I but had never taken out citizenship papers. He'd been a country fellow in Germany, and out here in rural Oklahoma, paperwork never seemed important to him. He was a practical man. He loved to hunt and owned several rifles and shotguns. In 1942, several FBI agents, in a routine check of registered aliens, went out to chat with him. The weapons made Doc Pfeiffenhauser look bad. The fact that he lived alone made him look worse. The feds searched for radios, cryptographic code books, and other spy goodies. They found nothing, which aroused even more suspicion. Finally, they carted our harmless veterinarian off to some camp — Camp Gruber, I suspect.

My husband, with his own Germanic and Swiss heritage, decided to get into the act. He rounded up a thick file of affidavits documenting Pfeiffenhauser's two decades of rural Oklahoma residence and professional contribution to animal health and food production. Pfeiffenhauser had never even visited Germany since immigrating.

What a party we had when he was released! We natural-born Americans were at first very apologetic, but Pfeiffenhauser was gracious, saying it was the best vacation he'd had in years. Even the food wasn't bad, he said. (I found that hard to believe.) Naturally he and my husband remained fast friends for years.

When I explained about Betsy over the phone, Doc Pfeiffenhauser rushed right over. Normally I would have let him handle the job alone. But I was so concerned about Betsy that I felt I'd better go along.

Doc Pfeiffenhauser drove his pickup across our rocky pasture to where Betsy was doubled up. The Doc looked Betsy over quickly. He tied a rope around her neck, then fastened it to a fence post.

I watched, dumbfounded and horror-stricken, as Doc Pfeiffenhauser tied another rope around the neck of the protruding calf. He backed up his pickup and tied the calf's rope to the hitch. Betsy never made a protesting sound. Doc Pfeiffenhauser eased the truck forward. Nothing happened. He backed up and gave the rope a little jerk. Again nothing. Then he backed up again and gave a big jerk. The new calf literally popped out. I was in a state of shock. Out flooded the afterbirth. It seemed like at least two barrelsful. The calf was in fine shape, and even Betsy seemed none the worse for wear. I was a complete wreck.

"Does this happen very often?" I managed to ask.

"Oh, I guess I jerk a calf every week or so," said Doc Pfeiffenhauser, calmly retrieving his ropes. He drove off with a friendly wave as my nerves slowly returned to normal.

One thing was now absolute — we would never again let Bill the Bull near sweet Betsy.

Big Red came in season again.

Hesitantly but dutifully, Gene informed Ritchie that Big Red was ready to be serviced. Susanna and Ritchie arrived the following morning.

We settled ourselves on the storm cellar roof. Ritchie poured Susanna and himself stiff shots from his ever-present flask. While our children were now free to come and go, the Fosses' children were conspicuously absent. Gene walked to the gate of the corral. Bill the Bull was already pawing the ground. There had been no rain for weeks and the dust cloud around Bill looked like a tornado. As a *professional* farmer now, I knew that dust kept the flies away — or at least helped.

When the gate opened, Bill charged out with a ritual snort as old as life itself. He rumbled heavily towards Big Red. But Big Red turned to face him head on.

"My God, what's wrong with Big Red?" asked Ritchie, gulping his drink. "She liked him before."

"This will be her fourth calf," I explained. "Sometimes after three or four calves, cows get harder to breed and turn just plain mean."

"Just like —" Ritchie started to say.

"Shut up, Ritchie," interrupted Susanna.

Big Red had always been difficult. Several times I watched her balk when my husband tried to lead her into the milking barn against her will.

Big Red and Bill the Bull did not actually clash horns. I would call it more of a face-off. Their heads touched all right — even bumped. But Bill was not going to spoil his chances by an all-out charge.

118

Instead, he merely tried maneuvering around. Big Red was in no mood to be maneuvered.

Gene realized the problem quickly. He was now expert enough to know that Big Red, despite her resistance, was truly in season. The breeding time is short. This weekend was crucial since he would have to go back to work on Monday. And worse, he knew that after an hour or two of this no-no game, Bill would be in a frenzy. He and Big Red might really do some damage to each other.

There was only one thing to do. Gene trotted to the barn and brought out his lasso.

"What's he going to do?" asked Ritchie urgently.

I had a pretty clear idea but didn't say anything. Gene twirled the rope like a real cowboy and easily landed a loop around Big Red's head. He started working her towards the loading chute. By this time Ritchie had capped and pocketed his flask.

"Hey, I see now," said Ritchie. He seemed serious for a change. After all, he would have a quarter interest in the calf. Ritchie decided he should help.

Before long, Big Red was secured in the ground-level end of the loading chute. Bill the Bull wasted no time in trying to take advantage of the situation presented to him. That's what Gene was counting on. Big Red, however, was determined to resist. Although Bill had his massive chest on top of Big Red's hindquarters, Big Red was using her final ploy. She kept her tail firmly clamped.

Ritchie was growing desperate. "Tell you what," he said to Gene. "I'll grab her tail and pull it to the side. Then you can give Bill a helping hand." As if Bill needed a helping hand!

Ritchie grabbed Big Red's tail all right. He gave a yank and then a heave — all to no avail. That tail stayed clamped. Ritchie was discovering just how powerful a cow's tail can be. Bracing himself, he gave Big Red's tail his most violent wrench. At this exact instant, Bill the Bull had no more inclination or ability to contain himself. Semen spewed all over the place. Big Red had won out over two men and one bull.

I looked at Big Red with sympathy. The calf was important to us, but my feelings were mixed.

Ritchie turned around. His face had taken the major portion of Bill the Bull's impassioned release.

"Great God, I feel like I'm pregnant," said Ritchie wiping at the sticky semen dripping all over his face.

I broke out laughing, much to Ritchie's disgust. I noticed Gene struggling for self-control as he turned his back on Ritchie and began fumbling with the ropes. Ritchie cleaned himself up and walked off, refusing to share his pet flask with anybody.

Ritchie and Susanna had had all the exposure to farm life they could stand. As soon as the war was over, Ritchie sold his share in Bill to us.

Back-to-the-basics just isn't for everyone.

SEVEN
THE CORN IS GREEN

During the war years, everyone with a piece of ground was urged to plant a victory garden. It would have been a minor act of treason not to have done so. But most of the topsoil had washed off our hill two or three centuries ago. We couldn't even grow grass.

With the moral obligation to develop a victory garden, my husband now had a convenient excuse to spend huge amounts of time with the Little Red Hussy, the seductive Sears tractor. With great diligence, he plowed at the acre or two in front of our house. After a couple of plowings, he announced that our garden was ready for disking. So he disked and disked, always with one boy or another in his lap. The boys learned how to shift gears, how the clutch worked, how to operate the choke, and how to kill the engine — all great masculine fun.

I planted lettuce, carrots, corn, okra, and radishes. The okra never sprouted. The lettuce rose out of the soil looking like wilted parsley, and the carrots never materialized. A few radishes did appear; radishes will grow in almost anything — even Alaskan tundra.

In late June I was inspecting my corn and managed to spot two diminutive green ears. I looked up to see a strange, old, rattly pickup chugging down our road. The cab was packed with kids. I could barely make out a man at the wheel and, among the children, a woman's face. They were Indians.

The woman disentangled herself from her brood and stepped out of the truck.

I ran to her with a scream of joy. She was one of my dearest friends from my PK past, Princess Mary. We had known each other since the beginning of my college life when my father was transferred to Heavener. Heavener is a small, remote town north of the Kiamichi Mountains, an area known for its solemn, lonely beauty. Princess Mary popped into my life during my first summer there, and we became devoted friends.

Princess Mary was a Cherokee. I never thought to question the princess part. She was an exquisite girl with lustrous, sparkling black eyes and long, black, beautifully combed hair. She had a rich, fresh, pale-olive complexion and stood poised and proud.

Like me, she played the piano, and we had great fun working on pieces for four hands. We also loved singing together. We were both sopranos and often sang duets in church. We quickly became the "twin Marys."

During that time, Princess Mary suffered through a terrible romantic crisis. She had fallen in love with a Creek boy. Her father, a chief, was furious; he would not allow Cherokees to mingle with Creeks. Her father sent her away to another part of the tribe to force a break with her Creek boyfriend. Princess Mary was living close to Heavener with Cherokee cousins when we met. She lapsed into severe depression and even our music could no longer cheer her. I returned to college and later heard that she had married Henry Bob, a father-approved, tribally approved, full-blooded Cherokee.

Princess Mary certainly seemed happy. Her four handsome, dark children were extremely well dressed in western clothes. Princess Mary was covered with gorgeous Indian jewelry. Henry Bob seemed prosperous and very much in love with his princess.

I shook hands warmly with Henry Bob, wondering why they had driven all the way from the other side of Muskogee to see me, especially in those days of rationed gasoline.

"We've had a dreadful time finding you," said Princess Mary, "but we need your help. I heard you'd married a smart lawyer. We're in trouble."

Henry Bob explained. "The sheriff and his men are after us. Not just Princess Mary and myself. They're after all the Cherokees."

I felt a chill creep over me as Princess Mary told their story. In World War I several Cherokees volunteered as a group. The American generals were quick to realize that the Cherokee language could be the perfect code. The Cherokee men were given radio training and sent to the front lines. The Germans may have known what was taking place, but they had no way of breaking the Cherokee code. From battalion to battalion, the Americans had safe, instantaneous communication because of the cleverness of those Cherokee men.

Their families in Oklahoma, needless to say, were concerned. On the front lines, the Cherokees were exposed to all the dangers of trench warfare. They needed the protection in battle that Cherokee braves had always enjoyed. The word was passed around, and once a month the Oklahoma Cherokees sacrificed a white chicken. The Cherokee radiomen returned home from the war without a single death among them. The tribe had expected that result. The sacrifice of a white chicken offers powerful protection, but the tribal ritual must be performed each month.

Somehow the Society for the Prevention of Cruelty to Animals — the SPCA — heard of these sacrifices. Since the SPCA had no legal authority, the mode of attack was through the sheriffs and deputy sheriffs in every county where Cherokees lived. The Cherokees — no strangers to persecution — were not willing to abandon the protection of their fighting sons on the front lines. They resorted to holding their sacrifices in secret.

When World War I ended, the Cherokees reduced the number of white-chicken sacrifices to one or two a year. But when World War II was in full swing, monthly sacrifices were again necessary. The Germans still had not learned the Cherokee tongue, and a new generation of Cherokee radiomen was in operation on the battle front.

One day near Tahlequah, in the heart of Cherokee country, a middle-aged man appeared on a bicycle. His complexion was fair, his hair, gray-blond. Germans ride bicycles and many are blond. When the bicyclist began asking the Cherokees questions about their language, the county sheriff clapped him in jail. The FBI descended on the case, and soon the fair-complexioned man was identified. He was a Yale linguist, too old for the war, innocently pursuing some obscure topic of research among the Cherokees. He was released and politely and firmly told not to publish anything until after the war.

Princess Mary and Henry Bob laughed over the story of the Yale linguist. Although any academic linguist could acquire a theoretical knowledge of written Cherokee — and certainly the Germans had such men — understanding the spoken language was an altogether different matter. Cherokee was used in fast-moving tactical situations. By the time a radio communication could be recorded, written out in phonetic transcription and laboriously translated by some professor, the battalion would have moved on.

"But we must protect our tribesmen," said Henry Bob. "Princess Mary has a brother at the front. I have a cousin there. We need you and your husband to help us sacrifice a white chicken."

I was intensely flattered — and confused. Then Princess Mary went on, "If the sheriff or somebody from the SPCA shows up, we need a persuasive defense. The sacrifices must go on."

"But how — "

"We know your husband is a lawyer and a good talker," said Princess Mary. "We're not certain what the white man's law says. One deputy sheriff has admitted to Henry Bob that he's not sure himself. Our defense can only be your husband's special arguments — one white man against another."

Now I was frightened. White men carry guns in the dense woods of eastern Oklahoma. I said I would talk it over with Gene.

Princess Mary and Henry Bob seemed enormously relieved. As we walked to their truck, they glanced at our meager victory garden. Before I could apologize for our paltry effort, Henry Bob said, "Too rocky up here."

"How well I know," I sighed.

Henry Bob smiled and hugged me before driving away.

"Of course we're going!" exclaimed my husband. "This is the chance of a lifetime! The ultimate honor!"

"What about guns?" I asked.

"Who said anything about guns?"

"What about the factory — the children?"

"I deserve a couple of days off — for the first time in 572 days — and so do you. Find a baby-sitter. Call Willy Wilson. You can take care of it, okay?" I glanced heavenwards for just a little assistance.

I found a baby-sitter. I called Wilson and asked him to take care of our animals. Feverishly we packed food, a tarpaulin, and extra clothes. I began to glow with excitement as we entered Cherokee country east of Muskogee. We drove through several small towns and finally reached the prearranged site where we were met by a group of Cherokees, members of Henry Bob's clan.

Princess Mary and Henry Bob greeted us with warm affection and asked that we follow them in our pickup. They led us to a remote clearing deep in the woods. We were near a lovely clear creek with willows hanging into the water. The other Cherokees arrived at carefully staggered intervals to avoid attracting attention. By late afternoon there were almost a hundred Cherokees, including children, all with big, black, somber eyes. The men wore overalls, as did a few women. Most women, however, preferred long print dresses with hems that swept the ground. Both men and women were wearing cowboy boots. I saw no feathers, beads, or moccasins.

Most of what I knew about Indian culture came from growing up in an Indian state. Forced to Indian Territory over the Trail of Tears in the 1830s, then cheated out of most of their land by white settlers, the Cherokees had suffered more than their share. My friends had survived on grit and pure spunk. Henry Bob was obviously a leader among his people, and I loved watching him walk from group to group with great assurance. Princess Mary told me that he'd gradually acquired several farms. His holdings were now so large that he hired other Cherokees to help him work the land. Princess Mary and Henry Bob's growing ambitions included sending their children to college. Another significant step for Henry Bob and Princess Mary had been their decision to join the Methodist church — but this did not mean that they would turn their backs on a Green Corn Dance.

Several men dug a huge pit, then started a slow, smoky fire. The women were dressing a whole steer that Henry Bob had donated for the occasion. When the steer was dressed, Henry Bob cut a hickory sapling, peeled off the bark, and worked it through the carcass. Six men hefted the steer and carried it to the pit. The steer was in for a twenty-four-hour smoke and roast. Various women took turns tending the cooking throughout the night and into the following day.

The sun set and the campground grew dark. The Indians built a small bonfire. Several women arrived with chickens plucked for cooking. The women spitted the chickens and began roasting them.

No one said a word. We ate the cooked chickens in deathly silence. I knew Indians had a quiet side, but something was very wrong. Finally Princess Mary explained, "Some of the men are afraid to hold the ceremony."

What could I say? Neither my husband nor I could offer any kind of guarantee.

The evening was long. People talked in low tones, but I was heartened by the fact that no one wanted to leave. Perhaps just being together was a source of strength.

Gene and I finally bedded down in the back of our pickup, fully dressed, under our tarpaulin.

"There can be nothing wrong with an ordinary Green Corn Dance," Gene muttered softly late the next morning.

Henry Bob remained silent for several moments, then said, "We will hold the dance."

The purpose of the Green Corn Dance was to thank the spirits of nature for the gift of corn. Princess Mary was busily roasting at least a bushel of green ears next to the steer.

The children spent most of the day playing a traditional Cherokee game called stickball. People were beginning to relax. Conversation was mostly in Cherokee, although enough people spoke to us in English to give us a positive and secure feeling about coming events. But no one was willing to mention the sacrifice of a white chicken.

At last the steer was roasted to the cooks' satisfaction, and we began eating early in the afternoon. We ate for what seemed like hours. I was so hungry, I gorged myself on the smoky, juicy beef. Perhaps being out of doors and in a strange situation added to my hunger. The feast was quiet. There was no wine, beer, or whiskey. We drank innumerable cups of good coffee, and I felt great. Conversation was still low key and sporadic.

An hour before dark, the men began lugging in whole trees and piling them in the center of the clearing. This was going to be a bonfire to end all bonfires! I wished my sons could see this spectacle. Although the Cherokees were not especially open or demonstrative, I could feel a communal spirit beginning to develop. I was intensely excited but controlled myself and attempted not to smile, which was surprisingly difficult.

A man was about to strike a match when I heard Henry Bob say something in a sharp, loud voice. Everyone froze including Gene and me. We could hear a pickup bouncing on the trail. The truck stopped at the edge of the clearing. A tall uniformed white man, a deputy sheriff, stepped out of the truck. From the other side emerged a large, middle-aged white woman. She was neatly dressed, as might be appropriate for a lady executive from Chicago or New York, even to brown oxfords and lisle hose.

Henry Bob looked at us. We both stood up and walked uneasily toward our unwelcome visitors. I could see in an instant that the deputy sheriff was uptight — in fact, he was scared stiff. His agitated appearance relaxed both of us, for now we had the advantage. There were too many Cherokees and only one of him, and I had the feeling he wished to God he was somewhere else.

The Indians were all impassive, silent, and very still. They simply stared, waiting.

"Oh . . . hello," said the deputy when he recognized we were white. "Looks like quite a powwow."

"A Green Corn Dance," corrected my husband.

"Seen any, uh, chickens around?" asked the deputy.

"We ate a whole bunch of chickens last night," I said brightly.

Gene turned slowly and glared at me. I glared back. My statement seemed logical to me.

"I'm Miss Hexford," announced the large woman. "Could I inquire how you killed the chickens?"

My husband impishly made a slit-throat gesture with one finger. "We axed their heads off," he said.

Miss Hexford winced slightly. "I see."

"This steer," said Gene, pointing at the skeletal remains in the pit, "was dead on arrival. But we did roast a bushel of live ears. You could hear those fresh, green ears crackling and snapping and protesting with pain — "

"Now see here, young man — "

"Now *you* see here, Miss Hexford. I'm an attorney-at-law. If you choose to interfere with this Green Corn Dance, I shall bring charges of illegal harassment and interference with religious freedom as guaranteed by the First Amendment!"

I wanted to cheer! My, I didn't know my husband could do *that*.

"White chickens have rights, too," retorted Miss Hexford.

No chicken so far as I was concerned had any rights. Obviously Miss Hexford had never taken care of a house full of squawking, fluttering hens.

"We haven't seen any white chickens," I chimed in sweetly. "Only Rhode Island Reds and some guinea hens. Should we be on the lookout for white chickens, particularly?"

The glare from my husband was less severe this time. Apparently my diplomatic endeavors were making progress.

"Sir . . . ma'am, I'm sorry about all this," said the deputy nervously. "We're under pressure — we have to check these things out."

"Nobody has any quarrel with the sheriff's office," Gene said. "To my knowledge, there has never been a false arrest in this county."

"False arrest?" exclaimed Miss Hexford. "They torture the white chickens first, then the children, then the women, *and then* — "

"Is it all right to *eat* white chickens?" Gene asked.

"Of course. It's only the torture that we find so immoral and unlawful."

"Unnecessary pain inflicted on dumb animals *is* a crime," Gene stated.

"Then you agree — "

"With the law, as written," said my husband.

I was dumbfounded. Gene was performing a Dr. Jekyll and Mr. Hyde, from merciless taunting to open reconciliation and even coddling. Miss Hexford was falling under the spell of my husband's smooth talk.

"Well . . . in that case . . . ." We chatted on for a few minutes. Then the intruders left; the deputy sheriff seemed especially relieved.

Henry Bob glanced at Gene, who said, "I doubt they'll return, but I can't guarantee anything."

Henry Bob walked toward the pile of wood. He took a match out of his pocket, struck it across the seat of his pants, and ignited a newspaper under some kindling. The Indians watched in silence. As darkness fell, the flickering light shone into their faces. I still did not know what to expect. Frankly, I was one big goose pimple. How could they be so quiet?

Suddenly I heard the throb of a drum. The dance was on! A hundred Cherokees — men, women and children — came to life. The heat from the fire was incredible. The sweat now poured out of everyone in double ration. I could feel it running down my back in rivulets. As people began milling around, a haze of dust rose up around the fire. At least I had known enough to leave my makeup at home. As the dust mingled with the sweat on my face, I realized I was becoming indistinguishable from the Indians. Princess Mary and I were again the twin Marys.

Through the dusty haze I could just make out the drummers. Six men, gathered around a large drum, beat in fierce unison. The songs seemed more like chants. The men chanted along with the beating of the drum, then all of a sudden there would be three sharp, heavy beats, and the chant was over.

The dancing was varied. A few of the teenagers pranced around the fire in an excited, energetic style, but most of the people were older. Their dancing formation resembled a long, slow-moving snake. Men and women, one behind the other, shuffled around and around the fire in time to the music. The entire body and psyche of each dancer seemed completely involved in the dance.

Princess Mary and Henry Bob invited us to stand up and dance. We did our utmost to imitate the rhythmic shuffle. No one paid any attention to us as we were absorbed into the pulsating snake moving around the fire. Before long we slid easily into the rhythm. The dust was thick upon us, and the sweat flowed more freely than before. If

Hitler could see us now, I thought, he would throw in the towel for sure.

After two or three chants we left the line and sat down. All at once everyone ceased dancing and encircled the huge fire. It was well past midnight. Little prickles ran over my skin as I realized that something important was going to happen.

Henry Bob emerged from the darkness near the drummers and moved to the fire. He had a live white chicken under his arm. Slowly he lifted the chicken aloft, and all was silent except for the crackling fire. Then Henry Bob burst into an impassioned speech in Cherokee. He held the chicken forward from time to time as if he were praising it. Abruptly he ended his speech with a high-pitched rhythmic chant.

There were no exclamations from the audience. I was keyed up and ready for an overwhelming burst of applause. I saw only a few nods of approval.

Another man, an elderly Indian, came forward and took the white chicken from Henry Bob. He proceeded to make his own speech, with a couple of fervent chants interspersed in his apparent praise of this fine, outstanding white chicken.

Speeches continued for an hour. Only men — no women — were leading the ceremony. Henry Bob stepped forward again. He spoke briefly, then opened a vein in the chicken's neck with a pocket knife.

The white chicken was released on the ground. It ran around in the crazy way chickens do when they have been beheaded, fluttering wildly as though in great pain. Blood splattered profusely over its clean, white feathers. I felt a little squeamish. Wasn't this "unnecessary pain"? Or was it just the same pain as when Myrtie wrung a neck or my husband or I chopped off a head with an ax?

Soon the chicken began to falter. When it fell over on one side, Henry Bob prodded it back up on its feet. He gave a short, loud chant. Again, it seemed that he was praising the bravery and valor of this fine white chicken.

The chicken was almost gone. Mixed feelings were swirling within me. I was caught up in the spirit of the ceremony, but I kept thinking, "Isn't some of this cruel?"

I watched the white chicken falter again. Henry Bob prodded it up for one last flutter of life. He repeated his last chant, then let the bird fall heavily forward to die.

There seemed to be enormous satisfaction, although no outpouring of response, among the hundred assembled Cherokees. The tradition was fulfilled. Sacrifice had been made for their young warriors' protection. I now found myself accepting the chicken's pain as indeed necessary. The group had been unified — had come together in one accord — seeking protection in the way of their ancestors.

In another few minutes the drummers took up a slow beat. Very gradually, several Cherokees returned to the dance.

Before long Princess Mary and Henry Bob appeared near us. Their mood was one of happy confidence. I saw Henry Bob hand my husband a small wad of something. Gene popped that something into his mouth. Henry Bob was chewing. Princess Mary giggled and told me they were chewing peyote.

After my husband had chewed awhile, he drifted into a kind of stupor and seemed to be hallucinating. I kept asking him what was going on but he was not very responsive. A number of Indian men were also chewing. The group grew incredibly quiet. Suddenly a Cherokee man leaped high into the air with a wild gesture and uttered a series of short staccato sentences. I could not tell whether he was uttering garbled Cherokee or speaking in "tongues." I presumed he was describing what he saw. He was extremely excited for two minutes, then lapsed into quiet peacefulness.

Gene leaped up at one point, but to my disappointment he had nothing to describe. Instead he became violently ill. Later he related that he had seen visions — brilliant, multicolored clouds.

"Just clouds?" I asked.

"Brighter than the aurora borealis."

"We've never seen the aurora borealis," I protested.

"It'll be a second-rate show if we ever do."

The Indians were accustomed to peyote and seemed to have great respect for its powers. One old man told us, "You can use peyote all your life and never learn all it has to teach."

Late the next morning Gene seemed steady enough to start packing our pickup for the return trip. Princess Mary and Henry Bob came to bid us farewell. Their gift to us was an overflowing bushel of green roasting ears.

"The Cherokees on the front lines are safe now," said Henry Bob.

"We'll write to my brother, and he'll spread the word," smiled Princess Mary.

We returned to our farm with a marvelous sense of well-being. We felt we'd made a great contribution to certain radiomen who had volunteered to enter the arena of modern warfare.

When we clattered into our driveway, Wee Willy was walking up the hill from the cowshed. He set down two pails of milk as we called him to our truck.

"Take some ears of green corn," offered Gene.

Willy helped himself. "These are right juicy-feeling ears," he commented, squeezing thoughtfully.

"They're Indian grown," I said. "From north of Heavener."

"Well, I didn't figure ears like these could come from this little garden here."

I looked at our dismal and ragged victory garden. What a waste of effort! When the Allies won the war, the Gubser garden would deserve no part in the glory.

In the search for men and women to work in factories, personnel managers gave everyone a chance. Deaf-mutes could not safely operate machines because danger is often heard before it is seen. But at visual tasks such as recovering reusable material and sweeping floors, these handicapped people were invaluable.

The blind could sort materials by feel. The deaf brought a blind person boxes of rivets that had fallen on the floor. The blind could feel which rivets were still usable and then separate the good ones by size; they were superb at saving hydraulic fittings, electrical components, and various fasteners and connectors involved in making planes.

Housewives from farms commuted to the factory. No doubt many of these women welcomed the chance to earn wages after the lean years of the Depression, but many simply wanted to do their bit for the war.

There was also a rough element, some of whom had been rejected by the armed services. Those factory workers often looked like barroom brawlers to me, but a crucial incident changed my mind.

Occasionally, when Gene had a few men over for poker, I would drive into town for an evening of bridge with the girls. It was a great relief to be with feminine company and talk about something other than pigs, cows, and chickens. Since I had that extra "tractor" gasoline, I picked up friends on the way in my 1936 black Ford. The Ford certainly was no limousine. The engine guzzled two quarts of oil a week, and a hole appeared in the floor under my feet. But the car kept running, and I poured oil into it and tried not to worry about the air swirling upward between my feet as I watched the pavement whiz past beneath me.

Late one evening, our bridge game over, I delivered my friends to their various homes and headed for the farm, wondering if I had won as much as my husband. Two miles from home I ran out of gas. I coasted to the side of the highway and set the brake. There was no service station open at this time of night. I knew the time must be near midnight because the change of shifts at both Spartan and Douglas was under way, with hundreds of cars streaming in both directions.

The only item of value I had with me was my engagement ring. I looked at the diamond for a moment, then slipped the ring off my finger and popped it in my mouth. Somewhere I had read this was the smart thing to do.

All I could do now was walk home, so I stepped out of the car and slammed the door. Suddenly one of those cars streaming by pulled over. Four huge men spilled out. I almost swallowed my ring.

"What's the trouble?" asked one of the men.

Carefully shifting the diamond to my right cheek, I burbled, "I'moutofgas." My heart was racing, and I knew they could hear the thump, thump. The four brutes glared at me.

"Okay," mumbled the leader. "Where do you live?"

I pointed in the direction of the farm, then said, "Twomilesthataway." I was discovering that talking with a ring in my cheek made me sound very funny.

"We're on our way to work, but we're a little early," said the man. "Get in your car. We'll push you."

"Ohboythanks," I gargled, scrambling back into my car.

I released the brake and waited tensely for the first bump. They maneuvered me into the traffic and down the road we went, bumper on bumper. We had to make a turn at the next intersection, then go another mile and make another turn into our little road. They continued to push me down the road, then into my driveway and right on into the garage. I jumped out of my car quickly and waved as they backed out our driveway and headed to work.

I discovered my teeth were still clenched. I gingerly opened my mouth and extracted my ring. I looked at it carefully, wiped it on the back of my pants, then slipped the ring back on my finger with a smile. My heart was only now returning to a normal rhythm.

I checked the boys. They were sound asleep, and so was my husband. There was no one to hear my story.

I undressed and slid into bed beside my sleeping husband. He seemed to stir, so I said, "I ran out of gas."

"Uhhmpf."

"Four men pushed me right into the garage."

"Ohhmmpf."

"But I took off my engagement ring and stuck it in my mouth. That was the right thing to do, wasn't it?"

"Uhh."

How nice to have a husband who cared so deeply about the perils his wife had just survived! I snuggled closer and soon was sound asleep.

To an authentic, born-and-bred, dyed-in-the-wool Oklahoman, there is nothing quite as hopeless as a lettuce-snapping, prune-picking Californian. Some members of that tribe are worse than others, but the absolute bottom of the pit, to my mind, were the Okies who emigrated to California and then had the utter gall to return. When they came back, they were different human beings.

A lesbian couple from California appeared one day at the Spartan factory and claimed to be a skilled riveting team. Skilled riveters were constantly in demand, especially for manufacturing airplane parts. The two women passed the usual security check and were hired on a trial basis.

Riveting was a widely used technique for joining two sheets of metal, usually aluminum. As the technique was then developed, two highly coordinated people were required to work together. One person operated an air-driven, hand-held riveting gun from one side, while the other handled the bucking bar that formed the completed rivet on the other. Compatibility was crucial to riveting teams.

The two lesbians were champion riveters. They were sensitive to each other's moods and capabilities. When a foreman announced a little competition, the two women always won the prize. There was admiration and there was disapproval. Whenever my husband heard of any harassment, he called the offending party in for a little patriotic speech. Despite moments of doubt and even cynicism about the war, the patriotic speech always worked.

Bob Wills and his Texas Playboys were in town, on tour to give plant workers a boost and a pat on the back. The band members set up their instruments right on the factory floor. Bob Wills said a few good words. Everyone laughed and applauded, then the music started and Bob sang. This was the biggest party ever held at the factory and the mood was festive.

The supreme test of tolerance for the lesbian couple began when the dancing commenced. I could hear the faint grinding of my husband's teeth. "Well, here goes," he said as the pair stood up to dance.

"What's wrong?" I asked innocently.

Before Gene could explain, a man approached the couple and tried to cut in. The older of the two women glared at the man and told him to get lost. Gene literally stopped breathing, and I wondered if I shouldn't take him out of the factory. Several people were watching eagerly, hoping for a showdown. I heard Gene exhale. The would-be Casanova shrugged his shoulders, moved off, and cut in on somebody else's girl.

Gene was in a thankful and diplomatic mood. He gallantly danced one dance with each of the two women, while the other hovered protectively. The rest of the evening flowed smoothly. "Those women are our best riveters," Gene finally confided to me. "I just hope they never try to steal anything."

When an employee was caught stealing red-handed, Gene recommended firing him or her without remorse, no matter how skilled the employee might be. In factories today, management often accepts — although not with good grace — the fact that many employees "absorb" tools and material for their own use. Workers are fired, as a rule, only if they start selling stolen material. Not so during the war.

In a specialized plant like Spartan, there was always an enormous array of expensive tools and materials lying around. As materials manager for part of the war, Gene was extremely anxious to keep hard-to-obtain items *inside* the factory. Frequently he would appear at the time clock at the change of shifts. Several hundred men and women would be in line with their time cards.

"Shakedown!" he would yell suddenly. Then he would step back and watch. Hundreds and even thousands of dollars' worth of tools and materials would bounce onto the concrete floor. Once on the floor, there was no way of identifying where the stuff came from. The foremen were assigned the job of cleaning up the floor and restocking the shelves.

The lesbian riveters never attempted to steal a thing. They riveted fuselages, wing sections, and tail assemblies until the end of the war. The enemy should have known better than to tackle such talented, dedicated people.

Gas Tank Gertie became Gene's bugaboo — a puzzling problem he could not solve.

By 1944-45, Spartan was operating at peak capacity with more than 3,000 employees. Gene was head of a management team consisting of six bright young men. Each man had a family and was safe from the draft because each was a vital worker in a critical war industry. This fact, of course, heightened their motivation to do a good job. Getty would say, "Look, men, we have a problem. I want you to do this, you to do that, and you to take care of . . . ." There would be a swift response, and the problem would be solved.

One day, Gene overheard two members of this elite group talking about Gas Tank Gertie. At the next staff meeting, Gene raised the question, "Who, or what, is Gas Tank Gertie?"

There was a moment of hesitation. Finally one of the men spoke up. "We're not sure who she is. We're not even certain she works for us. But she hangs out in the assembly bay where the gas tanks are welded together. She seems to conduct her business in that area. Apparently right inside a gas tank."

"What business exactly?" pressed my husband.

"Well, she's a prostitute."

"From California, I'll bet," said Gene, the Oklahoma boy.

Gene did not consider Gas Tank Gertie to be a joking matter. He ordered his staff to be on the lookout for her. While he rarely brought home his troubles from the factory, he seemed to think I could help — a dubious distinction, since I had never had one iota of experience as a prostitute or even with prostitutes.

"We need to set a trap for her," he mused.

"You need to identify her first," I said.

Several weeks passed with no developments. Then Gene again overheard men talking about her.

"Gas Tank Gertie struck again."

"Yeah. Got one of the machinists into a fight with a tool-and-die man."

"Sounds like a German agent to me. Isn't Gertie a kraut name?"

Gene decided to take personal action. He walked back to the assembly bay where the gas tanks were manufactured. He thoroughly inspected the entire area, then told the head of security to maintain extra surveillance. All the men assured him they would do their best. After all, a woman like Gas Tank Gertie could cause increasing disruption in the factory.

Again I listened to my husband agonizing over Gas Tank Gertie. "I don't see what the problem is," I said. "The men make good money. They can afford — "

"The problem is considerable," he said sharply. "She's already caused one fight. She's very likely a health hazard. Think of the men's wives. A situation like this can create severe morale problems."

Try as he did, he was never able to catch Gas Tank Gertie. She popped into conversations from time to time but remained a highly elusive professional hooker. I wondered if she operated with a look-out — and maybe a pimp. She probably had an entire staff. What a bankroll she must be accumulating!

Gene was not to solve the problem of Gas Tank Gertie for many long months.

War poster: The dirty, grimy infantryman stands glaring straight at you from a grisly battlefield scene. He looks as though he needs something — a gun or a jeep or a tank or an airplane — but *something*. He is waving his men forward. Enemy bullets are whipping overhead. You look again. It is painfully obvious that the soldier needs that crucial something right away.

Your eyes drop to the caption at the bottom of the poster. Printed in large block letters is, "Hell! I need it *now*."

The laboratory at Spartan used a variety of chemicals in testing certain critical materials. At one point, the chemists ran out of grain alcohol. They needed it *now*. The job of getting it fell into Gene's lap, along with a thousand other tasks. The usual approach to problems of supply was to figure out ways of pressuring people at various levels in the distribution system.

When the critical shortage of grain alcohol developed, Gene thought about the time it would take to wade through the red tape. He quickly decided to take another tack. Thoroughly understanding his home state of Oklahoma, he knew exactly where grain alcohol could be found. He called the sheriff of Tulsa County and asked if he had any 180-proof grain alcohol in his vault.

"We've seized a lot of 180 proof," conceded the sheriff.

"Is there some kind of court order that we can execute? I can provide any kind of language you want — technical, legal, patriotic. We need it right away at the laboratory at Spartan — in other words, for the war effort."

The sheriff paused for a moment, then said, "Come down to my office, Mr. Gubser. Wear an overcoat."

It was a typical Oklahoma August, and the afternoon temperature was at its high point, 102 degrees. Gene appeared at the house briefly, rummaged through the winter closet, and pulled out his best overcoat. There was no time for me to ask questions as he whirled out the door. I thought perhaps he was going to join the Russians defending Murmansk.

He drove downtown to the sheriff's office where he was escorted into the vault.

"All right," said the sheriff. "This shelf is 180 proof. Stick a pint in every pocket."

Gene did as he was told and began cramming his pockets with the state's evidence. "Don't you need a receipt for all this stuff?"

"Let's keep it simple," said the sheriff. "Don't tell anybody. Just walk back to your car as if nothing is unusual."

That command was a bit hard to accomplish wearing an overcoat filled with bottles of bootleg booze in the heat of summer. Nevertheless, Gene waddled out to his car sweating like a pig. With extreme care he drove back to the factory. The last thing he needed was to be stopped for a traffic violation and then be searched because of his ridiculously suspicious appearance.

When Gene arrived at the factory gate, he had still another hurdle. There stood a security guard with the usual strict orders to search each person. There was only one recourse. Gene never liked to pull rank, but the image of the desperate infantryman seemed to justify his action. "I'm in a hurry — search me next time." The guard valued his job, knew Gene well, and apparently was impressed by the urgency in Gene's voice. He waved him through with his contraband.

That evening we carefully inspected the sweat-stained overcoat. What a mess! The coat was completely stretched out of shape, especially around the pockets. The overcoat had been a rather extravagant gift from me. I had diligently saved quarters and half dollars out of the grocery money for months, and I was upset.

"Your contribution to the war," said Gene rather sadly.

"A brass plaque for a heroic overcoat," was my cryptic answer. Then I giggled. If one of those pints had broken, the powerful fumes might have caused him to wreck his car and be arrested for transporting an illegal substance. I could just imagine my silver-tongued husband trying to talk his way out of *that* one.

Rationing became a way of life for the wartime housewife. With American capability to produce both guns and butter, most of us coped fairly well. We heard of black markets on the East Coast, but using *agricultural* gasoline in my car was the extent of my dishonesty during rationing. Shoe stamps were often the scarcest. Before long, cloth shoes came on the market. Several of my women friends were delighted by such inexpensive and surprisingly chic footwear. Children and even infants were counted as full-fledged human beings by the government; consequently, we were issued stamps and coupons for five people. The boys preferred going barefoot during the summer, so that put me ahead on shoe stamps, which enabled me to trade with women who had no children. I saw nothing wrong with a little bartering and hoped the government didn't mind too much.

With sugar, butter, eggs, and meat closely rationed, a new social courtesy developed. If you had a sweet tooth, but did not care about butter, you worked out friendships accordingly. Since we had egg-producing chickens and milk-producing cows, I often brought pounds of butter, dozens of eggs, and pints of rich cream to bridge parties. In return I received canned fruit, sugar, and spices. Black pepper was one of the hardest items to obtain. Along with most housewives, I had to make do with only one container for the entire war.

My status as a provider of butter, cream, and eggs eventually grew to that of a celebrity. Even Polly Heddlestone began calling me to be a fourth in her bridge games, though she carefully avoided any mention of my husband. I still enjoyed Polly's company and included her when I extended invitations for an afternoon of bridge on the farm.

By the early summer of 1945, we knew the war was almost over. The Germans had surrendered, and the Japanese were on the defensive. Social activity was picking up, and I became quite a proficient bridge player.

Gene was out of town investigating possibilities for peacetime use of the factory. I invited Polly and six other women for an afternoon of victory bridge. We had an elaborate scheme for rotating everyone through the two tables.

School was out, summer was in full furnace force, and the children were running suntanned and barefoot over the prairie. The sound of war games, unfortunately, still resounded everywhere.

Lunch was served with two pots of coffee, after which Polly retired to the bathroom. She returned quickly to announce that our one and only toilet was clogged with dominoes. My sons rarely pulled tricks like that, and I was furious. Their timing was downright malicious, a blow below the belt, so to speak. I telephoned Willy Wilson and explained our plight. He agreed to come right over. When he walked in the door with an old sack of plumber's tools slung over his shoulder and an unlighted cigar hanging from his mouth, I was elated. Rescue! Our prince!

Polly had never seen Willy before. She said nothing, but her face showed her distaste.

Wilson, bless his tough hide, wasn't fazed in the slightest. He walked right into our bathroom, cleared out the dominoes, then gave the toilet a resounding, victorious flush.

"Kids will be kids," he rumbled, half smiling when he finished. Polly quickly squeezed past Willy into the bathroom without a word of thanks.

I chatted with Willy a few minutes, but he did not present a bill. When my husband returned, I would mention everything Wilson had done for us, and the two men would settle such affairs together. I never saw money change hands.

Willy was on his way out the door. The bridge players were beginning to settle down after this minor crisis. I stepped to the door with Willy. But Willy ignored me, which was not like him. All I could see was his short, broad back. He was breathing oddly.

"Willy. . ." I started to say.

Then I smelled it too. Our prairie was on fire!

The fire could have started in a thousand ways, but that was not our worry now. Whipped by the wind, a single flicker of flame could spread over dozens of square miles in a single day.

The last two summers had passed with no fires. That meant the fuel had grown and increased. The open prairie was now as dangerous as a mine field.

"Let's take a look," said Wilson.

Wilson and I rushed out the door, ignoring a chorus of protests from my bridge table.

Wilson and I climbed on top of the storm cellar, which gave us an excellent view to the north and east. The children stopped their play and joined us. I could just see the smoke.

"Looks bad," said Wilson. He licked his finger and held it up to the wind. "We're going to get it. Full blast. In about two or three hours."

"But it's miles away," I said.

"Don't matter. Three-and-a-half hours at the most."

"What —" I started to ask.

"If we hightail it out of here, we could be writing off the pigs and chickens and Lightfoot and maybe even the cattle. The smoke will choke 'em to death. And you forget the barns and your house 'cause they'll go up fast as a crumpled newspaper."

"What do you suggest?"

"I don't suggest nothing." *Where had I heard that before?* "It's a close-caller all right. But I'm going to stay and fight."

"Okay," I said, hardly thinking what this might mean.

" 'Kay. Call your husband's factory. Have 'em send out a whole bunch of men. Then tell those ladies in there to follow your kids into every barn in the neighborhood. I want every gunnysack they can find. I want you to round up every tub and fermenting crock and big kettle you've got. We're gonna set up right here in your front yard, 'cause your property is out here on the end of the line."

I ran back to the house. "Girls," I gasped, "the bridge game is over. A prairie fire is coming in fast, and it's a big one. I have to phone for some manpower. I want you to ask my boys to lead you into every barn near here and bring back stacks of gunnysacks. They'll know where to go."

"But why gunnysacks?" asked Polly.

"I can't explain now, Polly. We just have to do it. Willy Wilson is in charge."

I called the factory and, since my husband was absent, immediately talked to a man I knew I could trust. Had this been 1943 with the full pressure of the war on, his response might have been quite different. But now, in July 1945, there were rumors of orders being canceled at Spartan. He agreed to send men to fight the fire.

We were only two miles from the factory. The men would be arriving in minutes. I started gathering tubs, crocks, buckets, and kettles. Myrtie Wilson showed up with two huge washtubs. "Hiya, honey, looks like the crap done hit the fan. I reckon we're in for one hell of a party." My, how good it was to see her round face and strong 250-pound body! She had the kind of power and muscle we needed.

Willy Wilson appeared a minute later, dragging hoses from the neighbors' yards. We lined up the tubs and buckets and started filling them with water.

My bridge friends began drifting in with arm loads of gunnysacks. A gunnysack, or burlap bag, was then as much a part of farm life as barbed wire. The sacks came to the farm with feed in them, but none was ever thrown out when the feed was gone. Instead, they were kept in the barn or reused for all sorts of things — such as beating out fires. Sitting in the barn, however, the gunnysacks collected a lot of dust. My guests had all arrived dressed rather nattily for a bridge party. Their clothes were hardly chosen for fire fighting. But by now they had all seen the fire in the distance and had smelled the smoke.

Faces were grim with effort and concentration. Makeup was beginning to run with sweat. All the dust flying from the gunnysacks began to reveal wrinkles in my friends' faces I hadn't noticed before.

The first car of men arrived, followed quickly by a dozen more. In all, about seventy-five men were sent. I was happy to see every single one, for by now we could see the fire sweeping towards us.

I was put in charge of the women and my three sons. Our job was to soak the hundreds of gunnysacks we'd collected. Wilson picked out ten of the youngest men and assigned them the task of running the wet gunnysacks out to the fire line and bringing back the used ones for soaking.

Wilson rounded up several rakes and shovels, then organized the line. No one questioned his authority. He pointed out a series of fences to the men. They spread out forty or fifty feet apart.

In an hour we were ready. The runners started carrying the wet gunnysacks down to the men on the line. The smoke was billowing up in dense, gray clouds. Flames raced toward our neighborhood, but in an odd, scraggly way. Amazingly, there was no roaring inferno. The fire would engulf a large expanse of thin grass, then the wind would whip a swirl of embers across a creek or road or even an open stand of prairie. Some patches of flammable grass never caught fire. But overall, the front line of the fire was advancing at a ferocious pace.

If the fire did not directly threaten the animals, barns, and us, the thick smoke did. There was no way to avoid it, and I wondered how the fire fighters on the line could survive. Even before the fire reached the line, I saw men pull out their handkerchiefs and tie them around their faces. Willy must have suggested this action.

"Here," I said to a runner, "take this bucket down to the line. Pass the water along to soak the men's handkerchiefs. And for God's sake, keep those filthy gunnysacks out of this bucket!"

The fire reached the line. I could just barely see it through the smoke. The men beat at the fire until their gunnysacks dried out and began to smoke. Then a runner took the dry gunnysacks and gave the linemen wet ones. The shovels were more effective than the rakes. Most of the men instinctively saw where it was best to beat at the fire in their sector. But we certainly could have used another twenty men. A couple of men here and there began to falter as the smoke seared their lungs.

Suddenly a gust of wind blew the fire right through the line of fire fighters. A couple of runners stopped to beat at the breakthrough, but their efforts weren't enough.

"Wilson!" I yelled. He had seen the breakthrough. There was nothing more I could say.

"We've got to make a stand in front of the barns and the house," said Wilson, grabbing a couple of runners. "Women and kids too."

We armed ourselves with wet gunnysacks. Everyone was coughing now. The children's high-pitched little coughs were worst of all. But nobody had passed out yet.

Our women-and-kids fire line was a little ragged, but so was the fire. Flames shot up the hill right at us. The animals were skittish as

144

kittens on ice. Lightfoot and her filly, Miss Honey, were whinnying and racing around. The cattle were milling restlessly. If they stampeded, they would ram straight through any fence. The pigs were strangely composed, drat their conniving little brains! Those pigs knew there was no danger for them as long as we humans were willing to fight and protect them.

None of us was about to give up. I started beating at the fire for all I was worth. I kept my sons close by me and was astounded at how fiercely they were swinging those gunnysacks. My bridge-playing friends were doing just great. Myrtie whacked her gunnysack at the blaze with the strength and energy of two men. Wilson waded into the very heart of the breakthrough with a shovel and wiped square yard after square yard of flames right out of existence. To my astonishment, I saw Willy Wilson and Polly fighting side by side like infantry soldiers.

"You're doin' real good, ma'am!" boomed Wilson.

Polly looked at him kind of funny, then whack, whack, whack, she flailed away like a champion.

"Ain't never seen a city woman go to it like that!" shouted Myrtie through the smoke and fire. "Honey, you're the best there is." Polly smiled and kept right on whacking.

We stopped the breakthrough fifty yards short of the nearest barn. I had no idea it had come so close until a long, hard gust of wind cleared away enough smoke for me to see the blackened grass reaching toward the buildings.

The main fire line was holding well. Now the major task facing the men was to attack the suddenly flaring pockets of flame whipped up by gusts of wind. Even in our breakthrough we had a lot of mopping up to do to contain the smouldering fire. There was no rule to say this prairie fire couldn't flare up all over again at any moment.

We worked for two solid hours. By late afternoon the wind began to quiet as it often does in the evening. I saw one older man go down on his hands and knees hacking and coughing desperately. Wilson told a runner to drive him back to the factory to see a nurse.

Everyone was coughing and spitting. My bronchial tubes felt raw. The children, who loved to spit on any pretext, were having a field day. Wilson sounded like a solo trumpet as he cleared his throat and big chest.

I certainly was not above a good spit. Myrtie was the best woman spitter I ever saw. But the other girls were in agony. "Just imagine you're brushing your teeth," I told them. "Imitate the men."

Polly wound up her poor, exhausted face and spat.

"Good," I said. "We're all going to be spitting for days. If you have any pain, check with your doctor."

"I'll never smoke again," rasped Polly.

Wilson began releasing most of the fire fighters. He thought the neighborhood could handle any remaining patches of fire. I walked around shaking hands with all these wonderful men and assured them my husband would get a detailed report.

My eldest son, aged seven, came up to me and said, "That was the most fun I've had for the whole war." I hugged all three sons good and tight and expressed my delight over what good fire fighters they were.

An odd-looking pickup truck with a small tank of water, a hand pump, and hoses draped over the back entered our driveway. I saw the county emblem on the door. A man in a semblance of a uniform stepped out. Slowly, I walked over to the strange truck. I looked him straight in the eye. "I believe we have everything under control, sir," I said.

"Yep, looks good. Didn't want that fire to go any further. Any property damage?"

"Just grass," I replied, "thanks to —"

"Good. I'll fill in a report. The grass isn't worth much this year anyway. Call us any time you need help."

I watched the county officials drive off in their tax-supported pickup truck. Yippee! I thought ruefully. For this kind of help, people lost their farms during the Depression.

Gene arrived home the following day. I greeted him at the airport with singed eyelashes and a fuzzy smoked fringe across the top of my forehead — my worst wounds. He was crestfallen to have missed the biggest fire fight in ten years. He knew Wilson had saved the day, our farm, the house, the livestock, and the whole neighborhood.

"Your sons fought well," I said. "Their coughs are already a lot better, and you would have been proud of all three."

Gene nodded, pleased that there was so little damage.

"My bridge partners did pretty well, too. Even Polly Heddlestone."

Gene winced. To have his farm saved, in part, by that woman was a bitter pill. But fire plays no favorites. Actually I was rather pleased with the way everything worked out. Getting Polly together with Myrtie and Willy was my greatest social success of the war.

"Fill 'er right to the brim!" I exclaimed with an exuberant wave to a grinning service-station attendant. I listened happily to the gurgling sound of all that gasoline squirting into the tank. Then off I rattled in my old black Ford with a small can of white gasoline for the Little Red Hussy. Bless her sweet heart, she was beginning to show her age now with a few little wrinkles here and there, but she had performed beautifully all through the war effort. That one little piston never failed us.

The moment I arrived home, I gathered up the last of my gasoline stamps and tossed them into the trash. Then, laughing gleefully, I tore up my coupons for everything from sugar to shoes and threw the bits into the wastebasket. I never wanted to see rationing coupons ever again!

Yes, the war was coming to an end. I listened to all the great news on the radio, then I got back into my car full of gas and drove to the grocery store. Threading my way through the aisles, I ended up at the meat counter and chose an especially luscious pot roast — the boys' favorite. After selecting a vegetable, I remembered that we were out of bread and hurried to pick up a loaf. To my complete dismay, the shelves were totally empty. I soon found the manager, who explained that the bakery had gone on strike. Such a strike had been prohibited during the war, as everybody worked together for the cause. The war was indeed over, I thought. Now it's every man for himself. Well, coping with difficult circumstances wasn't new to me. I found some flour and yeast and tucked them into my basket beside the roast. I'd never in my life tried to bake my own bread, but today I would learn how.

Back home, I quickly stuck the roast and potatoes in the oven before calling our favorite bootlegger to order a bottle of Scotch. It was now time to make bread. I poked into several cookbooks and found the simplest recipe in *Better Homes and Gardens*. I then plunged into flour and yeast up to my elbows. Soon, I actually had a bowl of dough rising. Then I formed the dough into loaves — rather awkwardly — and before long, I popped them all into the oven alongside the roast. What an aroma! To my utter amazement, I soon had four golden loaves of bread. The boys and I sat right down and ate one whole loaf with homemade butter. Well, I would have to try this again!

The flood of good news made me euphoric. September 2, 1945, was declared V-J Day, and for several hours every human being in the United States seemed to be floating on air.

Just because the war was over, however, didn't mean that my husband would get home any earlier that day. It was a little past seven o'clock when I heard his old pickup chug faithfully into our front yard.

I'd never seen Gene look so exhausted. His shoulders slumped. His face was drawn. His brown eyes seemed gray. This was strange behavior for a healthy man just past thirty on the final day of the world's worst war.

"You look like you need a drink," I said, fighting to keep my bubbling self under control until I could find out what was wrong.

"Make it a triple," he sighed. I quickly fixed a stiff drink for him. He sank into his favorite easy chair.

My husband had never liked this war — never felt the fascination and enthusiasm that so many people did. While he couldn't stand Hitler, he saw World War II as a continuation of a European squabble — a serious one — that had started in 1914. "Maybe they wore themselves out for the rest of the century," had been his observation on V-E Day.

The Japanese were a different case. He was, I think, more opposed to and shocked by Hiroshima and Nagasaki than I was. He saw the defeat of the Japanese as their own mistake — they succumbed to militarism during the 1930s and 1940s when they should have stuck to business. Today, of course, the Japanese have largely accomplished — or, rather, exceeded — their goal of becoming a major economic force in the world. Perhaps their economic success since the defeat of militarism is a lesson for us all.

On V-J Day, I don't think my husband shared the feeling of moral vindication that victory represented for so many people. It was, instead, a hard day, for reasons I was about to learn.

"I had to fire the whole factory," he said at last. "Everybody's laid off."

It was inevitable, I supposed. I hadn't thought about it until now.

"This morning I had a conference with Mr. Getty. He started off by saying that as of today, there's no demand for what Spartan is manufacturing. So we have to start by laying off everybody. That's the new zero. 'Now, since I'm president of the company,' Mr. Getty said, 'I'll stay on. I need a factory manager. That's you. We both need secretaries, so that's employees number three and four. I want you to start from this new zero-plus-four and build up from there.' "

I listened somberly. I watched my husband take a long drink. I could see tears in his eyes.

"The men and women — they need their jobs," he went on. "Look at the work they've done for the last four years, how well they've worked together. They deserve something better than being fired."

"But haven't you been working on peacetime conversion?" I asked. "Don't you have some ideas?"

"Yes . . . ."

My husband did quickly hire back almost everyone who wanted to work. But the shock of that day was deeply ironic.

"Does that mean," I asked, "that you got rid of Gas Tank Gertie?"

That was the best thing I could have said. My husband began to laugh. "Yes, I did manage to ferret her out," he said, shaking his head. "When I gave my management team notice this afternoon, they came clean. They finally confessed that they'd invented a phantom hooker to plague me. Apparently it was screamingly funny for them to see me poking around the gas tanks looking for Gertrude."